The Black Mennonite Church in North America

1886-1986

The Black Mennonite Church in North America
1886-1986

Le Roy Bechler

**Foreword by
Joy Lovett**

HERALD PRESS
Scottdale, Pennsylvania
Kitchener, Ontario
1986

Library of Congress Cataloging-in-Publication Data

Bechler, Le Roy, 1925-
    The Black Mennonite Church in North America,
1886-1986.

    Bibliography: p.
    Includes index.
    1. Afro-American Mennonites.   2. Afro-American
churches.   I. Title.
BX8116.3.A37B43   1986   289.7'08996073   86-25691
ISBN 0-8361-1287-3

THE BLACK MENNONITE CHURCH IN
NORTH AMERICA, 1886-1986
Copyright © 1986 by Herald Press, Scottdale, Pa. 15683
    Published simultaneously in Canada by Herald Press,
    Kitchener, Ont. N2G 4M5. All rights reserved.
Library of Congress Catalog Card Number: 86-25691
International Standard Book Number: 0-8361-1287-3
Printed in the United States of America
Design by Gwen M. Stamm

91 90 89 88 87 86 10 9 8 7 6 5 4 3 2 1

A Five-Way Dedication

To the memory of James H. Lark, the first black minister and bishop of the Mennonite Church; to his vision and burden for the needs of the city and of his people; and to his readiness to risk and venture out in faith to meet these needs; to him, as a model for me of commitment to God's call.

To the memory of Rowena Lark, wife of James, and to the whole Lark family, for implanting that vision of service in me while I lived in their home during the summer of 1946 in Chicago.

To my wife, Irene, who as a partner with me dared to move into the ghettoes where we raised a family of three children and witnessed together the faithfulness of God's blessing in our ministry; to her insightful suggestions and readiness to peruse each page of this manuscript.

To the black members and leaders of the churches we planted and served; to their lives and our fellowship with them which taught us many lessons of God's love in cross-cultural relations.

To the Mennonite Church and the Home Ministries Division of the Mennonite Board of Missions which affirmed God's call in our lives over the years.

CONTENTS

FOREWORD

To deny a people their history is to deny them their worth, their identity, and therefore the possibility of belonging.

To give a people their history is to give them a future.

The black Mennonite Church is indebted to Le Roy Bechler, not only for his many years of service in pastoring congregations in Saginaw, Michigan, and Los Angeles, California, but also for his years of service to the Black Caucus of the Mennonite Church. His vision, insight, and participation have contributed greatly to the recent emphasis, within black and integrated congregations, upon evangelism, leadership development, and financial self-sufficiency. These are primary building blocks for the future.

In writing this volume Bechler has contributed a part of the foundation for understanding the future involvement of blacks within the Mennonite Church. He has taken the first step in recording the history of blacks in the Anabaptist-Mennonite stream, especially during the first half of this century.

Bechler has also cataloged the growth rate of blacks in the Mennonite Church through 1980 and has provided a brief biography of James and Rowena Lark. James Lark was the first black bishop within the Mennonite Church, and the couple was the first team of black church planters within the Mennonite Church. These stories have never been told.

Much remains to be done in analyzing the church planting and church development experience of the Mennonite Church in the black community. There are people, places and events not mentioned in this volume that come between the beginning and the present—a missing piece of the larger mosaic which may distort the total picture. This missing information is vital to the success of future efforts in the interpretation of black Mennonite history.

Not all who were a part of this development will agree with Bechler's interpretation or analysis. There will undoubtedly be those who will feel that another side of the story should be told, another point of view represented. This is a development to be encouraged rather than deplored as it will insure that additional pieces of the foundation for the future are laid. The history will become more complete; identity, worth, and belonging more firmly established; the meeting of black and white will be more of a family reunion than a gathering of guests in someone else's house.

Joy Lovett, Associate Secretary
Mennonite Church General Board
and staff person for the
Afro-American Mennonite Association

INTRODUCTION

This book grows out of my ministry in the black community as a church planter and pastor for more than thirty years. This experience has stimulated my interest in evangelism and church growth in cross-cultural settings. During these years God has continued to bring black, white, and shades between into that part of the Christian family called Mennonite. How did this cross-cultural church planting get started? What has God to teach us from a century of the black Mennonite story in North America?

This book deals briefly with the rise and formation of the black cultural movement and of the black church, reviews the inter-Mennonite experience in outreach to blacks (beginning in 1886), sketches a 50-year history (1898-1950) of Mennonite Church involvement in black communities, gives an overview and summary of the black response (1898-1980), and examines in depth the development of three indigenous black congregations in search of how the church can effectively communicate the gospel across cultures. John Bender compiled chapter three and wrote chapter four, "The Vision of James Lark."

Black and Anglo Mennonites have different yet similar histories, traditions, and concepts of Christianity and worship. In the history of the blacks, we see a people violently torn away from their homeland and forced into slavery. They suffered at the hands of a white folk who tried, yet did not succeed, to rob them of the Creator's image. This group walked through a wilderness, but God remembered them.

13

The history of the Mennonites, on the other hand, goes back to the sixteenth century. Mennonite forebears suffered severe persecution. They were hunted and tortured. Many fled for their lives from country to country in search of religious freedom. Interestingly, both blacks and Teutonic Mennonites came to the new world during the seventeenth and eighteenth centuries. As Hubert Brown asks in his book, *Black and Mennonite* (Herald Press, 1976), do these different, yet in some ways similar, pasts share a common heritage in a strange, new land?

The social and political ethics of the blacks and Mennonites had largely separated each group from the larger North American society. It was the civil rights movement in the 1950s and 1960s that brought about a greater mutual awareness among and interaction between the blacks and whites in the Mennonite Church.

In the 1950s the Mennonite Church spelled out its position on race relations. Mennonites took for granted that the church was open to all peoples and that they could participate fully within the church. It was not, however, until the late 1960s and in the 1970s that Mennonites made substantive attempts to reach blacks with the gospel and bring them into the life of the church.

The church now faced the challenge of meeting the needs and using the resources of its new minority members. This led to the establishment of the Minority Ministries Council, which became the Black Caucus, the Black Council, and more recently, the Afro-American Mennonite Association (AAMA). Their tasks were to assert that God was calling minorities into a fuller participation within the church.

Ethnicity and cultural awareness within society has had a profound effect upon the church as well. The dream for America to become a melting pot of all peoples never materialized. Ethnicity and multiculturalism remain hallmarks of the peoples of the United States and Canada. The church which seeks faithfully to speak and live the gospel in its setting today dare not forget its past.

In the succeeding pages I attempt to describe the emergence of black pastors and members in the Mennonite Church. Numerical growth has not been phenomenal, but there has been enough growth to indicate that God endeavors to build the church. What has helped and what has hindered Mennonite cross-cultural missions and ministry? What can we learn from the past that will help us extend God's kingdom now?

I am deeply indebted to the many pastors and individuals who have provided materials for this volume and who have provided counsel, encouragement, and most of all, inspiration by their ministry. I am also grateful for the encouragement of the Afro-American Mennonite Association, the Mennonite Board of Missions, and the Mennonite Historical Committee. I also want to acknowledge C. Peter Wagner who stimulated my church growth thinking and encouraged the research, and Dwight McFadden for his affirmation of this undertaking.

From these groups I have been privileged to work with an advisory committee which included Rick Stiffney from the Board of Missions; project coordinator Leonard Gross from the Historical Committee; Joy Lovett, associate secretary for Black Concerns of the Mennonite Church General Board; and Hubert Brown, former member of the Black Caucus and Historical Committee.

I am indebted to Don Ratzlaff for the story on the North Carolina Mennonite Brethren, the original 1886 mission. The article is condensed from *Mission Focus*, edited by Wilbert Shenk (September 1982). I also express appreciation to Arlene Miller from whose article, "The Brethren in Christ and Other Ethnic Groups" (*Evangelical Visitor*, October 10, 1982), I excerpted the Brethren in Christ history in black mission.

Mennonite Board of Missions has generously provided the services of word processing. I gratefully acknowledge their assistance. Special thanks is due copy editors Ross Lynn Bender and Shari Miller Wagner, Wilma Bailey who made suggestions for updating chapters 1 and 2, and all those unnamed who had a part in shaping this manuscript. It is a privilege to thank John Bender who has helped me put thirty years' accumulation of experience and learning into the story which unfolds in the pages of this book. I also thank Rachel A. Shenk for her careful work in compiling the index.

My prayer is that Mennonites will appreciatively understand and receive into the life of our church the rich contributions of the black religious heritage.

Le Roy Bechler
Sarasota, Florida

Rowena and James Lark

Pastors from black and integrated Mennonite churches at a leadership training seminar sponsored

James and Mattie Harris, church planters from Eastern Mennonite Board to Anderson, South Carolina. He died in January 1976.

by the Minority Ministries Council and Mennonite Board of Missions at Elkhart about 1975.

Michele, Leona, and Lee A. Lowery. His pastorates included Ninth Street Mennonite Church, Saginaw, Michigan, 1966-1981; Southwest Mennonite Fellowship, Chicago, Illinois, 1984-1985; and Bethel Mennonite Community Church, Chicago, beginning in 1985.

June and Hubert Schwartzentruber, long-time workers in St. Louis, Missouri. June died July 9, 1984.

Paul Angstadt, Jr., has served the Buttonwood Mennonite Church, Reading, Pennsylvania, since 1981.

The Mark Lehmans, St. Anne, Illinois, associated with the Rehoboth Mennonite Church. Left to right (back): Michael, Mark, Pauline, Christine; (front) David and Maria.

1
THE BLACK CULTURAL HERITAGE

One of the most significant events of modern times has been the rise of the black cultural movement in the United States. American blacks for generations have faced obstacles in developing and defining a coherent cultural identity. The attempted deculturation of blacks began during slavery when they were taken from their African homeland, stripped of their cultural roots, and forced into a life of servitude. To justify and defend slavery and the slave trade, many whites argued that the Africans were cultureless savages. The white culture made every attempt to stamp out any evidence of African culture.

As a result of this ruthless assault, the majority of black Americans rejected Africa and anything related to their African heritage. It was to them a source of shame, which led them to reject their blackness. Malcolm X clearly understood this when he proclaimed in 1965: "We have been a people who hated our African characteristics. We hated our black heads, we hated the shape of our noses ... for we hated the color of our skin."[1]

The slave sought outwardly to identify with the dominant white culture the best he could whether by assimilation, acculturation, submission, or any means that would allow him to survive under difficult circumstances. His role, however, as a piece of property with few or no rights left the slave caught between his African culture and the vise grip of white society. As Malcolm X observed, "This loss of any distinctive cultural identity ... was made worse by the unwillingness of white society to recognize and accept the Afro-American as a part of the dominant culture. In these circumstances many blacks found themselves in a cultural limbo without an adequate self-image."[2] James Baldwin addressed the self-identity problem in a speech made in 1963. He said, "A black child born in this country ... discovers two terrifying things. First of all, he discovers that he does not exist, no matter where he looks—by which I mean books, magazines, movies, there is no reflection of himself anywhere.... [If] he finds anything which looks like him, he is authoritatively assured that this is a savage, or a comedian who has never contributed anything to civilization."[3]

This tendency of white America to ignore the personhood of blacks led to stereotyping God's created as inferior and subjecting them to segregation. At the same time, Christians failed to relate the gospel to the situation of being black in a fallen society. The struggle for liberation from white oppression—in society at large and in the churches—would take this people on a torturous yet certain road to victory.

Identity confusion

What sense of self-identity did the black man and woman have who rose out of slavery? Dr. W. E. B. Dubois interpreted the black struggle at the turn of the century and tried to delineate the role of the newly emancipated black person in America at a time when blacks were neither accepted nor fully understood. He wrote in 1903:

> One feels his two-ness—an American Negro, two souls, two thoughts, two unreconciled strivings, two warring ideals, in one dark body. The history of the American Negro is the history of this strife— this longing to attain self-conscious manhood, to merge his double self into a better and truer self.... He would not Africanize America, for America has too much to teach the world and Africa. He would not bleach the Negro soul in the flood of white Americanism, for he knows that Negro blood has a message for the world. He simply wishes to make it possible for a man to be both a Negro and an American without being cursed and spit upon...."[4]

In retrospect, blacks did Africanize America, especially in the south. Southern culture reflects African culture, for instance, in speech patterns, friendliness, hospitality, and respect for elders. Contemporary studies point out that much more of African culture was preserved than was earlier believed.

As important as the Civil War and the reconstruction era were to the evolutionary aspects of black culture, the times left much to be desired in making adequate strides for the newly freed people. Progress came as a percentage of freed slaves pursued an education and began to work for meaningful change. Freedom became the goal of the black struggle.

What whites believed to be true of blacks has had some bearing on what the blacks themselves perceived. White American culture had a crippling effect on the attempts of the Negro American to cope and in their new setting to do what all people everywhere must do if they are to develop fully—find an identity, a sense of worth, relate to others, love, work, and create. The miracle is that blacks do love, work, and create in spite of 300 years of oppression. The evidence abounds in the poetry, songs, music, preaching, friendliness, and love that are present in the black community.

The great American dream saw society as a melting pot of all peoples. The individual was expected to gain an education and job, become acculturated, and then be assimilated into a pluralistic, multiracial society where race would make no difference. Many believed this possible—that human identity would transcend all ethnic or racial identity. However idealistic that hope was, the black person's dilemma remained fixed: the black was not really considered worthy of the melting pot mix.

The frustration, anger, rage, and pain of being treated as nobodies gave rise to a new black awareness movement that created near panic across the nation. Not until the Martin Luther King, Jr., era and the later civil rights movement, did black Americans begin to enjoy the fruits of the freedom won over a hundred years earlier. Nor has the melting pot melted. Today we see how the African slaves helped create a new society, a new culture that was partly African and partly European.

New black awareness

What was this new black awareness all about? It was the black quest for an authentic black identity, an identity which would help them come to terms with themselves as persons. The impoverishment of blacks in northern urban ghettos may have created the identity problem more than the earlier history of slavery and emancipation.

Black awareness now essentially dealt with the right to self-determination, racial pride, and the recognition of the vitality of blackness or black culture. To be black meant to be oneself, to have an identity, to be a person in one's own right.

In the mid-1960s a number of blacks began to realize that the civil rights movement did not offer an effective solution to the identity crisis or to the whole problem of cultural marginality. "One of the weaknesses of the civil rights movement was that it offered no cultural program other than the integration of blacks into the dominant white culture, and the implications of this type of integration were greater than a growing number of those blacks were prepared to accept."[5]

For an increasing number of blacks, including King, integration implied only the superiority of everything white and the inferiority of everything black.

Civil rights only granted certain rights. Blacks were given access to white schools, white residential areas, white institutions, white culture, and white values. Yet in the process they were denied their own racial identity as well as their African heritage. The most outspoken critics of the civil rights movement, Runcie says, went so far as to condemn integration as a "subterfuge for the maintenance of white supremacy."[6] They dismissed it as a form of genocide which destroyed black institutions, denied the existence of a separate black culture, and effectively absorbed the qualified black elite while doing nothing for the community as a whole.

The insight of these critics, or prophets, changed the course of the black protest movement. The emphasis began to center on the distinctiveness of black culture and the virtues of black lifestyles, along with the value of black consciousness. This shift in emphasis dealt squarely with the negative self-image so prevalent in the black community and thus encouraged a stronger racial solidarity.

The cultural renaissance that developed in the late 1960s had its roots in various twentieth-century movements—most notably the Garvey Movement, which attracted much support after World War I. Its champion, Marcus Garvey, preached a powerful doctrine of black pride, racial solidarity, and African nationalism. He exalted the strength, beauty, and superiority of blackness and emphasized the culture and history of Africa as an additional source of pride for the American Negro.

The Garvey Movement's influence spread widely. The resulting cultural ferment captivated black poets, writers, and artists. Their work, often militant, expressed the search for a genuine ethnic identity. They drew on material from the black folk culture and African heritage. In an essay published in 1926, Langston Hughes wrote: "Most of my own poems are racial in theme and treatment, derived from the life I know.... It is the duty of the younger Negro artist ... to change through the force of his art that old whispering 'I want to be white' ... to why should I want to be white? I am a Negro and beautiful!"[7]

The foundation gradually emerged, then burst into view for many to see. No other concept of the civil rights struggle so caught the imagination of the black community as the dawning of its own black identity.

The new awareness continued to revolutionize black society. As blacks gained an appreciation for their racial identity, they came to realize that to gain human dignity and individual development meant getting power. "Black power," an ideology that emerged in the mid-sixties, rests upon a concept called Negritude—a positive statement of racial pride and identity. The "black" aspect of this ideology seeks not to elevate blacks above others but to raise them to a position of equality with all other races. Beyond mere identity, Negritude provides an emerging symbol of common unity and cultural experience.

Significance of the black cultural movement

Never before had white America been brought face to face with its hypocrisies. As long as the slave labored in chains, the Declaration of Independence and the Constitution symbolized the ability of American whites to lie to themselves. Having lived so long with this lie, whites found it difficult to resolve the contradiction between equality and discrimination once slavery had ended. An awareness of the glaring discrepancy between the belief in freedom and equality and the practice of discrimination against blacks ultimately touched the sensitivities of many American whites. The black cultural movement pinpointed the issues. The sins of past years came up for public judgment.

The new awareness revealed racism as a cancer eating away the dignity of compatriots, both white and black. The public came to see racism as the unwillingness of white Americans to accept blacks as fellow human beings. Authors and psychologists Grier and Cobbs, who served on the National Advisory Commission on Civil Disorders, cited the root cause of urban riots as that of white racism.

The sixties was the decade of Malcolm X and Martin L. King, Jr., of the beating of participants in black sit-ins, and of freedom riders in the South. Black children risked their lives for so-called "integrated" education. The lonely struggles of voter registration and the bombing deaths of innocent children finally brought about major changes in the laws. The legislative, administrative, and judicial systems helped break down the legal barriers that had dealt such grave injustice to a downtrodden people.

Runcie in his analysis of the black cultural movement points out several significant facts:

> First, the African heritage was loosely interpreted and effectively exploited as a potentially rich source of ethnic pride. . . . Their version of the African heritage was frequently over-simplified, distorted, and ar- tificial, but it did furnish a valuable fund of imagery, symbols, and myth. The central symbol was blackness itself. Identification with the pride and beauty of blackness was held to be inconsistent with the use of the term "Negro." As part of the re-emphasis of the African heritage, Negroes were transformed into Afro-Americans or Blacks.[8]

With the rising emphasis on African history, the study of Swahili became popular. This represented an effort to form a tie with the mother country. There were other African-derived symbols of racial pride such as the wearing of dashikis, bubas, and caftans. The most universal symbol however, remained the "natural" or "Afro" hair style. Other forms of African lifestyles were introduced and practiced on a limited scale. Some blacks changed their names to rid themselves of a slave master's legacy.

During this period black studies were introduced as the black cultural renaissance swept through American schools and colleges. The movement prompted the rewriting of many school texts to better reflect the contributions of all minority groups.

Then, too, the recognition and promotion of "soul culture" constituted an important contribution to the renaissance. Soul culture embraces every aspect of ghetto life. Barbara Am Teer has described it as "the way we talk ... the way we walk, sing, dance, pray, laugh, eat, make love, and ... the way we look."[9]

The symbolism and mystique of "soul" effectively promoted a sense of identity and solidarity among its users. Terms such as soul food, soul music, and soul brother along with songs such as, "Say it Loud: I'm Black and Proud," echoed this new black consciousness.

The black cultural movement in the mid and late seventies focused more and more on the meaning of black liberation. Many of the groups within the black communities engaged in the struggle for fuller realization of freedom for their people. Some advocated a strict separation, while others took a less militant approach.

What of the future? What of this movement's ebb and flow? Whatever lies ahead in the black cultural movement lies ahead for black and white alike. The journey has begun. As Jesse Jackson says, "We are less likely to be put back into white slavery. We are better equipped intellectually, emotionally, and technically to protect ourselves. We finally had to come to that independence to get to the next step."[10]

2

THE RISE AND FORMATION
OF THE BLACK CHURCH

It is well known that the black church within the North American context played a significant role in the development of the black community in the United States. In fact, the black church has been a bulwark of spiritual and moral strength; it has provided a social structure for a people who were denied access into the dominant culture. Probably no other institution played a more important part in the lives of this people than did the church. This cannot be sufficiently understood without going back to the beginning, to when blacks were captured in Africa and transported to the new world as slaves.

The following section traces the role of religion in the development of the black church, its status, and some of the ways in which it has made an impact upon the black community as well as upon the nation.

Uprooted

In the early 1600s traders with an eye for a lucrative business brought slaves to the American colonies. These slaves, most of whom came from West Africa, were snatched by force from kin and home and were usually the youngest and fittest males. Some time later, females were added to the slave trade.

Once captured, these people found themselves confined to stockades or concentration-like camps without regard to sex, family, or tribal affiliation. After sale as chattel to slave dealers they were packed into the holds of the slave ships for transport across the ocean. Again, they received treatment only as cargo, without regard to sex, age, clan, or tribal difference. This was but the beginning of a process by which blacks were stripped of their social heritage and, to a considerable degree, dehumanized.

One of the slave owner's first tasks involved breaking in his "property" to the plantation system. This required a certain amount of regimentation. The slave master tended to ignore social bonds among blacks and to destroy any of the traditional social cohesion they might have had. Both the organization of labor and the system of discipline on the plantation tended to prevent the development of social cohesion based on whatever remnants of African culture might have survived and on the slave's role in the plantation economy. The problem of communication added to the dehumanizing process and made necessary the learning of a new language and the adjustment to a totally different way of life.

The black slaves had been abruptly torn away from the traditional African system of kinship and other forms of social interaction which had given security and meaning to their lives. They were now at the mercy of the dominant culture which bought and sold them as animals. It was under such conditions that blacks struggled to establish roots in a strange land.

The Africans received little or no religious instruction in the New World. "Do they really have a soul?" some asked. Most whites answered evasively or in the negative. Since an unwritten law said a Christian could not be held as a slave, the exploiting class opposed any proselyting.[1] As time went on, however, religion became a means for controlling the slaves. It was a widely held belief that religion sustained rather than threatened slavery. "The gospel is our mightiest safeguard," a Charleston minister explained, "for it governs in secret as well as in public; it cultivates the conscience and thus establishes a more vigilant watch over individuals' conduct than Foucher himself ever accomplished by his unrivaled police."[2]

The slave masters used Christianity to perpetuate a slave theology in a slave culture. In so doing, whites lost the transcendent symbols of human worth and substituted temporal symbols relating to the doctrine of humankind. While the slave masters were using religion as a means of perpetuating and easing the effects of slavery, the slaves were also finding a solace in religion.

African heritage

In the eighteenth century a vast majority of slaves practiced whatever fragmented rituals from their African past they could remember, though these were often modified by the suppressive life on the plantation. Some maintained that the African tradition was lost in slavery, but in the black Christian experience aspects of the past culture were still evident, including the tradition of storytelling and story told in song.[3]

In the midst of slavery the blacks could not have survived without a worldview that gave some meaning to life. Mitchell confirms this when he says:

> No group or race suffering the oppression and brutal treatment heaped on black Americans could possibly have remained, for the most part, healthy, sane, and productive without such a strengthening world view as blacks brought with them from Africa. It was the angle of vision from which all great joys as well as sorrows were seen. For life to continue to be worth living, some sense had to be made of it; some interpretation had to be given to the absurdly cruel and unexplainable experience that they were undergoing. The spirituals are eloquent testimony of how far the slaves were from blissful "ignorance" of the injustices done them. No matter how scientifically naive or politically powerless, they were aware. And this awareness would have driven them crazy en masse had they not brought with them a way to view and affirm life when things hit them hardest.[4]

Christianization efforts

Prior to the Revolutionary War there was a conscious effort to Christianize the slaves. The Christian faith offered salvation and spiritual security to all persons regardless of their status in life. Yet most black slaves never became church members. Since the black church was suppressed, it is hard to estimate how many were Christian prior to the Civil War.

The slaves who accepted Christianity were well aware that those who taught them did not really practice Christian doctrine themselves. The realization is reflected in the well-known spiritual which says: "I got shoes, you got shoes, all God's chil'un got shoes. When I get to heaven, I'm goin' to put on shoes, but everybody talkin' 'bout heaven ain't goin' there." No doubt the slaves had in mind the white masters who were harsh in their treatment of the slaves. From the sociological viewpoint, the spirituals represent, along with what Frazier

calls "the invisible church,"[5] a basis of unity for the black community.
As John Lovel (McKinney) says:

> The Negro ... analyzed and synthesized his life in his songs and
> sayings. In hundreds of songs called spirituals, he produced an epic
> cycle, and, as in every such instance, he concealed there his deepest
> thoughts and ideas, his hard-finished plans and hopes and dreams. The
> exploration of these songs for their social truth presents a tremendous
> problem. It must be done, for as in the kernel of the *Iliad* lies the genius
> of the Greeks, so in the kernel of the spiritual lies the genius of the
> American Negro.[6]

As the black church began to emerge, it was not uncommon for
slaves and masters or for freed Negroes and whites in the cities to worship together. There was, however, a movement against slavery that
was beginning to make its voice heard in the North and was affecting
the slave institutions of the South. The religious institutions began to
feel the impact which was to bring divisions to several major denominations.

In 1787 two free black ministers, Richard Allen and Absolom
Jones, were worshiping in the St. George Methodist Church in
Philadelphia, a congregation in which blacks were regular participants. These two men were kneeling in pews, but in the wrong
pews. During prayer they were abruptly escorted to the "nigger
pews." As a result of this indignity Allen and Jones, along with other
blacks present, left the church permanently. In 1816 Allen established
the African Methodist Episcopal Church.

As more freed blacks assumed spiritual leadership, numerous
black churches were formed between 1800 and the Civil War. Slaves,
too, began to preach to fellow slaves under the watchful eyes of the
masters.

During this period, whites began to have second thoughts about
teaching religion to slaves. They feared that blacks would develop a
spirit of freedom and grow to resent their imposed status. The fear
intensified when in 1831 Nat Turner led an insurrection in Virginia.
The discovery that Nat Turner was a preacher led to what contem-
poraries called the "Dark Days" of Negro religion.[7] Although at one
point religion began bringing black and white people together, the
lines of separation were drawn prior to the Civil War.

It remained for the Civil War to finally break down the institution of slavery. Blacks developed a slave culture within the imposed white structure, but on the whole they were forbidden to form any type of social organization or structure that would lead to their independence.

The black church after emancipation

Following emancipation the "invisible church" which had grown up among the slaves merged with the institutional church of the blacks who were free before the Civil War. This resulted in the rapid growth of the organized black churches. Franklin Frazier points out that the importance of this was the structuring and the organization of black life to an extent that had not existed before, because "(1) all organized social life among transplanted Negroes was destroyed by slavery; (2) the traditional African clan and family was destroyed—nor was another permitted to develop in the New World; (3) efforts to organize religious services were prevented because of fear of slave insurrection; (4) the slave's role in social structure was uncertain, other than his work-related role; (5) little organized social life structure was permitted."[8]

The black church became a potent social force within the black community. It not only provided a social structure, but it also was a means of social control. One of the most perplexing problems following emancipation concerned the black family and sexual practices. Under the slave regime, family and permissible sex relations were structured under the supervision of the black master. But the church began to censure unconventional and immoral sexual behavior and to punish by expulsion sexual offenders and those who violated the monogamous mores.

The black church established economic cooperation with the black culture by organizing Mutual Aid Societies. The first of these, the Free African Society, was organized in 1787 by Richard Allen and Absolom Jones. Its purpose was to be a brotherhood, sharing and giving support to one another in sickness and for the benefit of widows and fatherless children. Many of these beneficial societies were organized in the cities as well as in the rural areas and were generally connected with the church.

During slavery the religious life of the slave community brought diverse people together and provided a sense of meaning to their lives.

In the church, McKinney says, they found a basis of unity; here they found the emotional support which the conditions of slavery required.[9] It is understandable that worship during this period had a strong element of emotion, for this provided a needed release from the tensions which developed in their day-to-day experience. Following the Civil War to the present, the black church has performed much of this same function.

After reconstruction, the lines of segregation began to be drawn sharply between the blacks and whites. The lines were so distinct that the church became the only institution where blacks could give expression to their deepest feelings and, at the same time, achieve status and find a meaningful existence in a hostile white world.

Because the church was the only institution that was not controlled by whites, religion took on a central function in black life. The church automatically became a social force to help blacks deal with economic, political, and social problems they faced. The black minister became the respected community leader. The church was (1) a place where blacks could aspire to become leaders; (2) a place where individuals could achieve *distinction* and symbols of status; (3) a place to struggle for power, where the thirst for power could be satisfied; and (4) a place where men could assume the dominant role.[10]

With the beginning of the civil rights movement, the church played an even more powerful role. The church became the central location for community meetings. In cities across the land where protests were held, people went nightly to the church for announcements, directions and, more basically, spiritual and moral renewal.[11] The success of these protests owes a great deal to these churches and their leaders.

The black church or religion has had a profound effect upon the black community. In fact, blacks and the black church cannot be understood apart from their history. Basic symbols that have emerged in the past decade probably show the relationship most convincingly. Jackson refers to black as "soul," a symbol illustrating that blackness is a beautiful gift from God.[12] The raised arm with closed fist also illustrates this idea and was the symbol of the black power movement. A particular handshake indicates to another the solidarity of spirit— brotherhood.

In general, black power is rightly interpreted to mean the

development of a sense of racial identity and solidarity by black people in order that they may more effectively achieve their goals in America. Broadly speaking, black power is to be equated with the kind of mutual cooperation and support which all minority groups, ethnic or religious, have practiced in America.

When blacks were not permitted to be a part of the white church nor the social structure of the predominate white society, it was the black church that became the springboard enabling them to find meaning and purpose in life.

3
BLACK BEGINNINGS AMONG MENNONITE-RELATED GROUPS

Mennonites, from their earliest decades as immigrants in a new world, were aware of the presence of blacks within the colonies. In 1688, they, along with some Quakers, lodged a formal protest about the handling of men as cattle, noting there is no more "liberty to have them slaves, as it is to have other white ones." Something of this attitude continued over the centuries, even though there seems to have been no thought of Mennonite evangelism that would reach out to these blacks.

To be sure, Mennonites during their first two centuries in North America were German-speaking, by and large. General Mennonite interest in the Great Commission would not surface until after the Civil War era, when the English language slowly but surely came into its own as the mother tongue of more and more Mennonites. Mission interests arose, simultaneously.

Mennonite mission among the blacks finally began in North Carolina, in 1886, the outreach of the Mennonite Brethren Church. The Mennonite Church baptized its first black members in 1897. These and other accounts of black Mennonite beginnings, as presented below, help set the stage for an understanding of later historical developments of the black Mennonite movement.

Mennonite Brethren Church

Perhaps it was the distance that prompted the Krimmer Mennonite Brethren of Kansas and South Dakota to label their fledgling outreach in the Blue Ridge Mountains of North Carolina as foreign missions. More likely, admits J. A. Toews in his book, *A History of the Mennonite Brethren Church* (1975), "the concept of missions among the Krimmer Mennonite Brethren (as well as among most Mennonite groups in times past) has been determined not only by geographical distance, but also by color of skin."

Nevertheless, when the Krimmer Mennonite Brethren opened their mission work in the poor black mining community of Elk Park, North Carolina in 1886, they blazed a trail for all Mennonite groups. Historian Harold S. Bender credits the KMB Conference with starting "the first Negro Mennonite work."

The North Carolina work had its beginning in the missionary vision of a woman named Emily Pruden. Pruden had established a number of schools for white and black mountaineers in the northwestern part of the state. Finding her schools understaffed, she sent out a call for Christian teachers to come teach among the mostly poor country people.

The Krimmer Mennonite Brethren heard the call and sent Heinrich V. Wiebe and his wife to a school in Elk Park. Since North Carolina law at that time forbade the mixing of white and black children, two schools had been established in the community, one for each race.

Miss Pruden acquired the property of the black school, a lovely eight-acre orchard plot on a hillside overlooking the town, without problem—only because the racially hostile people were unaware of her intentions. The KMBs eventually acquired this school for the conference.

With the arrival of the Wiebes, the intent of their mission—to reach the black population for Christ—became clear, but not without repercussions. Area residents, not blessed with the missionary burden of their new KMB neighbors, recoiled from the thought of whites operating a mission for blacks. They made life difficult for the new workers from the Midwest.

After the Wiebes' first day of teaching, the locals made their feelings known. Mrs. Wiebe found a note on the front porch with a scribbled message: "We the citizens of Elk Park will not allow for a white man to stoop so low as to teach the niggers, they have enough of their own color to teach them. Your time is up! After this day."

Recounting many of their experiences in the *Christian Witness,* the KMB periodical, Mrs. Wiebe reported that after "taking the matter to prayer," they resumed the work as before. In the months that followed, she added, "Brother Wiebe received a lot of persecution, such as being called names and being thrown at with rocks, but he was never hurt in any way."

That almost was not the case. On another occasion the stubborn courage of the Wiebes came to a near-fatal climax. As Heinrich Wiebe was returning home one evening, he hurried to cross a railroad bridge which spanned a deep and foreboding draw. Halfway across, Wiebe stopped short at the sight of familiar—and angry—townspeople armed with sticks and clubs emerging from the brush to block off both ends of the bridge. Warned of his imminent death, a "fall" into the deep draw below, Wiebe asked his tormentors if he might have a word of prayer. Thinking the request harmless, and perhaps taking some sadistic pleasure in hearing this "nigger lover" plead for his life, the neighbors obliged.

Wiebe knelt solemnly on the tracks, clasped his hands tightly, closed his eyes, and began to pray. To the surprise and apparent chagrin of his captors, there was no prayer for deliverance. Instead, Wiebe began to pray fervently for each person by name (he recognized them all) and asked God's blessings on their families and his mercy on their souls. When Wiebe muttered the final "amen" and opened his eyes, the vigilantes, perhaps duly admonished by the sincerity of the prayer or simply worn out by its length, were nowhere in sight.

The work continued unimpeded and, after a year, took an unexpected direction with the arrival of a number of homeless black children. One child arrived so undernourished, reported Wiebe, "that he got ill after he had eaten a square meal. After he had been with us a few days he said, 'Isn't this a nice place? I can have all the oatmeal I want.' "

As more children came to the Wiebes' door, the missionaries asked their sponsoring board for direction. They were given permission to open the doors wide, and in 1903 the board sent two more workers, Jacob M. Tschetter and his wife. Cramped for space, Heinrich and Jacob cut down trees around the place. With the lumber they built an addition which doubled the size of the building and included a chapel and living quarters for the orphans and the two missionary families.

It wasn't long, however, before the building, with its capacity for 20 children, was again crowded. The Tschetters and the Wiebes could accept only the most needy children between the ages of three and 12, and care for them until they were 16 or 18. "Oft times the work was hard and we could not progress as we should due to limited means," wrote Mrs. Wiebe. "These were pioneer days for the [KMB] conference as well as for us."

Sarah Wiebe Heinrichs, Wiebes' daughter, recalled the animosity of local whites toward the growing work. On one occasion, a noisy group gathered outside the orphanage and shouted for her father. He refused to appear. Eventually the mob left, but not without leaving their calling card—a large pile of rocks on the front porch, evidently ammunition for an assault.

Another time, some of the boys from the orphanage were walking past the home of a policeman's girlfriend. "I think it's going to rain; I see dark clouds coming," taunted the policeman. One of the boys retorted, "And I think it's going to snow; I see white clouds." Before the night was out, there was a warrant out for the youth's arrest. He quickly packed his bags and fled the state.

In time, the area mines shut down. With the community cut off from its economic lifeline, many of the blacks moved elsewhere to find work. The Elk Park orphanage was eventually closed, and the ministry followed the migration to the new promised land, Lenoir. The orphanage still stands, abandoned and nearly buried by trees and brush; nevertheless, it is a monument to a daring vision of compassion and outreach.

Peter H. Siemens and his wife were two other leaders who aided in the emergence of the North Carolina churches. They arrived on the scene in 1925. They were alumni of Tabor College, Hillsboro, Kansas, the Bible Institute of Los Angeles, and Moody Bible Institute. The Siemens couple served for more than 30 years among the mission churches and were the guiding forces in their formation as a conference. Under their leadership, the North Carolina work extended "over a radius of 60 miles, from the eastern tip of Tennessee into the heart of the Blue Ridge Mountains," wrote J. A. Toews. Eleven churches emerged, and Siemens served as their superintendent for many years in addition to his teaching and preaching ministry. Siemens is credited with founding a high school for blacks, said to be the first of its kind in western North Carolina.

Under Peter Siemens' tutelage, ten indigenous ministers were ordained to serve the churches. Among them was Rondo Horton, who has given leadership in his several decades of conference activity. In his mid-80s (at this writing), Horton remains the dominant figure in the life of the churches. He served as moderator of the conference from the mid-1950s, when the Siemenses left, until his retirement in 1972. After a brief stint as a retiree, he returned to take the moderator's post in 1978.

The North Carolina District of Mennonite Brethren churches today includes: Laytown; Bushtown, Bush Hill, and West End in Lenoir; Newland and Darby in Ferguson. These churches make up a conference of about 260 in membership. Except for a small church in Chicago, the North Carolina churches are the only Mennonite Brethren churches east of the Mississippi River.

Mennonite Church

The first black members of the Mennonite Church, as far as is known, were Robert and Mary Elizabeth Carter and their son Cloyd. On April 21, 1897, they became members of the Lauver Mennonite Church, Cocolamus, Pennsylvania, a congregation in the Juniata district of Lancaster Mennonite Conference.

In a letter to the author, Raymond C. Lauver from the Lost Creek Mennonite Church reports that a class of 32 people was taken into membership at the Lauver congregation on April 21, 1897, including Robert, Mary Elizabeth, and Cloyd Carter. "A number of the class were listed as husband and wife," Lauver writes, suggesting something had changed the traditional practice of young people joining an instruction class and being baptized before marriage.

Indeed, a spiritual awakening had come to the area as the result of a Sunday school conference which some members attended in 1895 at the Blough Mennonite meetinghouse at Hollsopple, Pennsylvania, in the Southwestern Pennsylvania Mennonite Conference (later the Allegheny Mennonite Conference). Three persons, all from Juniata County, responded there to an invitation to accept Christ as Savior, writes Clayton A. Graybill in the *History of the Lost Creek Mennonite*

Church (1962). "This was the spark that aroused the ministry to contact others that needed to be challenged with the claims of Christ for the forgiveness of sin." The visitations resulted in thirteen additional confessions. This group was baptized on January 1, 1896.

Through the initiative of a lay person, evangelists M. S. Steiner and A. D. Wenger were invited to hold meetings at the Lauver church during the following winter, 1896-97. "This was during the time evangelistic meetings were begun and they were permitted to be held three nights only at a place," explains Raymond C. Lauver. The interest continued beyond the first three evenings although, because of the opposition of some in the congregation, the evangelists had to confer with the bishops in Lancaster County before proceeding. In a letter dated February 19, 1897, A. D. Wenger informed fellow evangelist S. F. Coffman in Vineland, Ontario, that "the bishop, Wm. Auker went to consult headquarters in Lancaster County to get these meetings stopped." Services continued in five other locations in the community, each for three nights.

A. D. Wenger reported to Coffman that "more than fifty precious souls have professed Christ as their Savior. Some forty odd are affiliants for membership. Among them are three or four past sixty years of age, a number in middle life, and three Negroes. The Negroes are affiliants for membership, perhaps the first for our church." Though Wenger does not give their names, we know from other accounts that these were the Carters.

One of the meeting places for the evangelistic services was Rockland School, located on a corner of the Lauver farm. The Carter home was located "on another corner, about one-half mile away," Raymond C. Lauver, says. "As a boy I well remember Cloyd and taking him to church sometimes as well as taking milk and other food to him sometimes. He was crippled and later in life he was cared for in a home in the community."

Robert and Mary Elizabeth Carter are buried in the Lost Creek Mennonite Church cemetery. She died on November 24, 1906; he died on August 12, 1912. Their son Cloyd for a time lost fellowship with the church. However, around 1920 he was restored into fellowship. Cloyd (October 13, 1878—March 22, 1949); Mary, his wife (August 21, 1882—June 2, 1912); and their daughter Viola (age 14 years) are buried in the Lost Creek cemetery.

Brethren in Christ Church

For much of Brethren in Christ history, contact with persons of other ethnic backgrounds was limited. Carlton Wittlinger in *Quest for Piety and Obedience* (1978) notes that references to American blacks in early Brethren in Christ records are sparse. Because the early Brethren in Christ were northern, rural people, they only incidentally encountered black Americans. The Philadelphia Mission reported the baptism of the first known black member in 1907.

Not until the civil rights struggles of the 1960s did the denomination as a whole show interest in black Americans. At that time, Wittlinger notes, "The *Evangelical Visitor* broke out in a rash of articles on race." When two black families who attended a south central Pennsylvania congregation moved to the New York City area, interest was stirred to begin a ministry in Brooklyn.

In the 1950s several black families and many children and young people began attending the Valley Chapel congregation in Canton, Ohio. Although blacks and whites in equal numbers have worshiped there for nearly thirty years, it was only a few years ago that the first black person was elected to the congregational church board.

In the mid-1970s the Brethren in Christ began to support financially two black churches in Philadelphia—Christian Stronghold and Southside Center. Pilgrim Chapel, located in Brooklyn, is the only totally black Brethren in Christ congregation in North America. Together black membership in these churches has now reached a total of about 100 persons.

General Conference Mennonite Church

Before World War II the General Conference Mennonite Church had no mission work among blacks. Beginning in 1950 the newly reorganized church, through its board of missions started work among blacks by supporting interdenominational missions. The first such support was given to the East Harlem Protestant Parish, started in 1949 by a group of pacifist students at Union Theological Seminary.

Attendance and reception of blacks as members of General Conference urban congregations occurred by another route. Jobs brought a rapid rise in the number of people moving into the northern industrial cities following World War II. Blacks were among those who came. As the larger black urban population began expanding out of earlier ghettos into formerly all-white neighborhoods, many whites and their congregations fled to the suburbs.

Second Mennonite Church in Philadelphia stayed in its location and served both blacks and Puerto Ricans. First Mennonite Church in Chicago stayed in its neighborhood. Woodlawn Mennonite Church in Chicago, began as a Sunday school for children of the new Mennonite Biblical Seminary in Chicago (since 1968 located in Elkhart, Indiana, as part of Associated Mennonite Biblical Seminaries). Woodlawn became the first organized church in the General Conference to have interracial membership and integrated pastoral leadership. Among those serving the congregation was Vincent Harding, the first black church leader in the General Conference.

Other General Conference urban congregations moved to the suburbs; one joined with a Mennonite Church congregation.

Bringing blacks and members of other ethnic groups into General Conference membership, not part of the initial mission strategy, encouraged a new sense of Mennonite identity. The identity was no longer based on ethnic definitions, but on a new fellowship of people who "could worship together, respect old traditions, create new traditions, and build a new family of God based on a common faith," says Lois Barrett in *The Vision and the Reality* (1983). "They could untangle and retie faith and culture in such a way that culture was an invitation to faith rather than a barrier."

Beachy Amish Church

The Beachy Amish Mennonite Church began mission work among blacks in Washington, D.C., in 1965. The mission grew into the Fellowship Haven congregation located on Douglas Street in the northeast part of the city.

The witness began as a joint endeavor of Amish Mennonite Aid and the Missions Interests Committee, both agencies of the Beachy Amish Mennonite Church.

Work began with children's Bible classes and progressed into summer Bible school, Sunday school, adult prayer breakfasts, Sunday evening open-air services, camping, a government-funded children's program, and regular church services.

In the *Amish Mennonite Aid Mission Report, 1955-80*, compiled by Andrew Hershberger, former and founding pastor at Fellowship

Haven, Elmer J. Lapp, writes, "The small congregation is assuming various responsibilities and desires to continue relating with the larger Amish Mennonite groups as well as become a much greater force for God in the lives of more people among the masses of the city."

Conservative Mennonite Conference

Mission with blacks in the Conservative Mennonite Conference grew out of Voluntary Service involvements. In the late 1960s the conference mission agency, Rosedale Missions, sent Raymond Byler to Jackson, Mississippi, to give leadership to a fellowship intended to serve VSers and former VSers who stayed on in that city.

The fellowship developed into the interracial Open Door Mennonite Church. It became an autonomous congregation in 1978. Tom Horst serves as pastor since the retirement of Raymond Byler.

A mission effort with blacks in Louisville, Kentucky, has been under discussion by the conference. A support couple for a time held Bible studies in their home in west Louisville.

Some blacks attend the Louisville Mennonite Church in the southeast part of the city. The area, however, is mostly populated by whites. The Louisville congregation, too, grew out of Voluntary Service involvements there.

Retrospect and Prospect

In the story of the Carters above, it was noted that they were buried in the Lost Creek cemetery. Writing in the Lost Creek congregational history Raymond C. Lauver refers to the congregation's "mission-mindedness in spite of inconvenience and handicap." Clayton A. Graybill adds, "This was before the days of 'prayer meetings' in the Mennonite Church but not the days before Christians prayed. Fervent prayers were sent heavenward by young Christians in behalf of their sinner friends and older folks especially for those that spent many years in sin."

No reference is made in the Lost Creek congregational history to the Carters, but the reader gains a sense of the context in which the spiritual awakening was taking place across the entire Mennonite Church. The Carters, as well as other black and other minority members of the Mennonite Church to follow, would still need to see further changes come in their adopted church before they would be regarded as familiar equals to those who traced their ancestry to Mennonite, Amish, and Hutterite families in Europe. The spiritual kinship was not a point of contention; getting into the Mennonite family circle sometimes was.

4

THE JAMES LARK VISION

The guest room in the home of Le Roy and Irene Bechler in Inglewood, California, became home for a visitor who had taken ill in mid-
April 1976 on a business trip to Los Angeles. James H. Lark had come
as an observer to a meeting of the Allensworth Advisory Committee, a
governor-appointed body working on a proposed state historic park
and reconstructed black settlement.

Founded in 1908, the community of Allensworth lay between
Los Angeles and San Francisco, seventy miles south of Fresno, where
Lark made his last home. Allensworth had been financed and
governed by black Americans. It was dedicated to creating an environment to meet the critical need of psychological emancipation for
blacks, who just 45 years earlier, in the Emancipation Proclamation of
January 1, 1863, had been freed from the physical institution of
slavery. The black founders intended Allensworth to be a community
where blacks would develop free of the direct influence of slave-
oriented social attitudes.

The community grew rapidly in the first years. The Caucasian
land development syndicate, however, from whom the California
Colonization and Home Promotion Association had bought the land
for the pioneering community, did not live up to its agreement to
provide a water system equal to the needs of the community. After
1925, residents found it increasingly difficult to develop further the
agricultural and ranching industry without more water. Residents
began to leave or seek employment in other industry. Those who

stayed made adaptations in farming and sought other business, too. Some drilled their own wells. In 1966, however, dangerous levels of arsenic were found in the drinking water. A brief historical sketch of Allensworth says: "With the prosperity of the town diminishing, its hope of community lessened."

On May 14, 1976, the State Park and Recreation Commission approved plans to develop Colonel Allensworth State Historic Park, an important first step in giving rebirth to a community that had been slated to be plowed under for agricultural development. James Lark, for a time a resident of Allensworth, was a driving force for reconstruction of a living community, more than just a park, that would demonstrate the enduring experiences and contributions of blacks.

James Lark had the concerns of Allensworth on his mind when he came to stay with the Bechlers. "I wanted to have a church in there," he said. "Some fainthearted individual said we can't carry it." But he saw a spiritual vacuum, and longed for "ministries that would meet a need at Allensworth."

Lark's sudden illness brought him into the company of friends. Brother Lark, as he was invariably called by those who ministered with him, more than 25 years earlier had been instrumental in bringing the Bechlers into ministry in the black community. The five days he spent in their home became an occasion for recalling the events, ideas, and people who figured closely in Brother Lark's ministry. The first black bishop in the Mennonite Church, Lark was still talking "plant, personnel, and program" as the essentials for keeping the church moving forward with black brothers and sisters. To him a church without movement was a church without vision.

Lark likened his role in the church to that of a tugboat. The even-keeled, rural-oriented Mennonite Church must have appeared to him as a barnacled vessel, reluctant to follow the new currents charted in black mission. The church was pouring its resources into overseas mission, reserving only "rowboat" efforts for mission at home, he believed. Lark and the mission workers he called into service at home helped steer the Mennonite Church into a larger mission among blacks. Would the white church venture still farther into the new waters and discover blacks as brothers and sisters with gifts as well as needs in church planting? Would Mennonites, black and white, accept the vision of their black bishop?

Lark tugged at the church to respond to the post-World War II mission opportunities among first generation black émigrés to the cities. His vision and drive led to mission starts and related program developments in more than six locations. The partnership in ministry of Rowena Lark, his wife, gave stability, grace, and strength to their effective outreach. She was particularly gifted as a soloist and children's storyteller. For James to recover from the experience of her death in 1970 required a spiritual experience parallel to conversion, he said in the 1976 reminiscing.

James Henry Lark was born on May 4, 1888, in Savannah, Georgia, the son of Lela and James Lark. His early experiences had a profound effect on his life and were propelling forces in his ministry. Orphaned at age six, he knew what it was like to be alone and poor. He saw the oppression of blacks and witnessed the lynching of an uncle by a hostile mob.

Lark attended the Baptist church as a boy, was baptized at the age of 16, but did not continue to participate as an adult. He attended the Quaker Institute for College Youth at Cheney, Pennsylvania (now Cheney State College). After graduation in 1916 he taught at the Florida Baptist Academy in Jacksonville. He took further training at the Washington (D.C.) Normal School, followed by more teaching and service in the Armed Services during World War I. In 1918 he married Rowena Lark. She, too, had been a student at Washington Normal School, living with an uncle and aunt of her husband-to-be. They were married the day before James shipped out to France.

A sergeant in the medics, Lark served overseas for two years. He recalled hearing General Pershing tell the soldiers, "Wars aren't won in bed." He had vivid memories of discrimination against black soldiers, and he developed health problems from exposure to gas. Lark was placed in the TB hospital for two and a half months, but further diagnosis showed that he only had the incipient form of the illness.

The Larks lived in a number of places following his discharge from the service, including Quakertown, Pennsylvania. Here the family occasionally attended a black Baptist church. They lived on a farm adjacent to where the Rocky Ridge Mennonite meetinghouse would be built in 1949. The church began in 1931 as a mission of Franconia Mennonite Conference. The workers were Mennonite young people with a deep desire to reach out to the unchurched. The group at first met in homes, rented buildings, and mission halls. Mission workers Linford Hackman, Abram Landis, and other young fellows picked up the Lark children for Sunday school. An aunt visiting from Florida attended a service at Rocky Ridge and recommended to Rowena that she try out the congregation. Rowena was now teaching in Washington, D.C., 160 miles away, commuting home on weekends.

Just as with the children and Rowena, James' first direct contact with Mennonites was with members from Rocky Ridge. Lark recalled the wintery Monday morning Linford Hackman and Abram Landis stopped by his house. They asked him to go with them up the mountain to help two elderly men who had been snowed in for nearly a week. Their example of bringing food, chopping wood, and then bringing their spouses to help with cleaning and laundry made a deep impression on him. At home he went upstairs to think about it all. "How could I condemn them?" he remembered thinking. He started going to the Mennonite church regularly from then on.

Lark was a member of the American Legion in Quakertown. One evening he said to the moderator, "I have a statement I want to make. I have joined the Mennonites and, as of tonight, I'm resigning from the American Legion." One of the members who had not heard the whole statement got up and said, "Now hear, I don't want no pussyfooting on this thing. I want to know who offended or said something against Jimmy Lark." The moderator said, "Nobody said anything against Jimmy." The man said, "Well, what's he resigning from among us for?" The moderator answered, "He has joined the Mennonites." The fellow's only response, Lark said, was "Oh," and he sat down. James Lark had given public notice of a new direction in his life. That fall of 1935 the family left the farm to move to Washington.

The Larks joined the Brentwood Mennonite Church in Cottage City, Maryland, established in 1922 as part of Lancaster Mennonite Conference. When James joined the congregation, the pastor told him: "I'm not going to require you to put on the plain coat, but I want to say this to you, if you wear the plain clothes you will receive spiritual blessings and be blessed otherwise."

Lark added, "Well, I couldn't see that, but I however consented to wear plain clothes. When I went downtown to do business, though, I'd take the plain coat off."

In 1936 Rowena was asked to help in summer Bible school work in Harrisonburg, Virginia, the beginning of a wider church ministry for the Larks. In 1943 the Larks were asked to assist in Bible school work in Chicago, Illinois. The attendance and interest was beyond expectation. The Larks transferred the enthusiams for the weekday Bible school sessions into a regular Sunday morning worship service. Before returning home they organized a group to continue the new mission effort. The following February the Larks returned to Chicago to serve in the leadership of this mission which was to grow into the Bethel Mennonite Church. Here James Lark was ordained minister on October 6, 1946, and bishop on September 26, 1954.

Lark believed that spiritual and financial power needed to be put in the hands of black churches. He saw the inaction of the white church on behalf of minorities as "falling down on the job." He was exasperated with the slow response of the church. "The time has come when the blacks in America have got to stop wringing their hands and going to the whites with a smile full of teeth begging for things," he said. "Backed up with spiritual and financial power, the blacks need to say, 'This is a program that we think should be in operation.' " He said the church needs "to get it together" in dealing with its attitudes, and move to action because "there've got to be changes made."

Time after time he came up with proposals to help the black church "turn over a new leaf." Lark, Le Roy Bechler, and Melvin Leidig are mentioned in the one-page "Minutes of a Meeting at Bauman's Garage," probably in Goshen, Indiana, in 1951. The intent of the meeting was to discuss a proposed plan concerning a "Colored Evangelism Committee." Lark presented a tentative constitution. Such a committee, the group agreed, would "solve problems that would not otherwise be understood and solved properly," and would "unite Negro Mennonite churches." The conferees decided to take up the matter with another city mission pastor, Vern Miller. They noted a caution in the minutes in that they "thought wise not to present it to the Mission Board [Mennonite Board of Missions, Elkhart] too soon."

Mission secretary and friend J. D. Graber wrote in a May 31, 1976, letter to Le Roy Bechler after visiting Brother Lark at Veterans Hospital in Chicago: "He has always been characterized by a consuming vision that just drove him on and on to keep expanding the kingdom. When he was in Chicago years ago he said he would like to convert all the black people of Chicago and build them into a Mennonite church. This kind of vision has been characteristic of him and I found the fire still burning in his bones."

Lark liked to say, "You can't get ahead as long as you're trying to catch up."

Lark was a foundation builder. He systematically assessed new opportunities in existing urban congregations and drew up proposals for creative, if ambitious, action. He saw what could be done in unchurched urban areas to reach blacks. "How do you hold back a person who's ready to put a church in every city in the United States?" says Le Roy Bechler of his friend and mentor. "James Lark was fifty years ahead of his time," Bechler adds.

The Lark vision helped start churches in black communities in Sarasota, Florida; Youngstown, Ohio; Saginaw, Michigan; Los Angeles, California; and in other communities. He brought a new awareness churchwide for the needs within the cities. At the same time he drew on rural resources for the benefit of urban mission. Mennonite camping programs in Ohio and Illinois are outgrowths of his pioneer efforts in expanding ministry with boys and girls. He wanted program, trained workers, and adequate facilities, not what he called guesswork, timidity, or delay in urban mission. His gifts lay in conceptualizing and getting outreach efforts started, a task that included dealing with seeming mountains of obstacles.

While serving as pastor at Bethel in Chicago, the Larks were instrumental in planting the Dearborn Street Mission as an outpost. During the same time Brother Lark bought ten acres of land at Hopkins Park, Illinois, for a camp. The Rehoboth Mennonite Church of St. Anne emerged from this effort. In St. Louis, Brother Lark did the legwork for what later grew into the Bethesda Mennonite Church. During retirement in Fresno, California, he bought a church building there and began services. He sold the church when the Southwest Mennonite Conference could not come up with a pastor. He helped in a number of other churches and wanted to see a church established in the Allensworth reconstruction project. At one point he was asked to serve as interim pastor of Calvary Mennonite Church in Los Angeles. His leadership came at a crucial juncture in the life of the congregation as the population of the community was changing to mainly black.

After the installation of Le Roy Bechler as pastor at Calvary, Lark later moved on to serve as an interim pastor of the Zion Mennonite Church in Wichita, Kansas, a congregation struggling for life. He developed both short- and long-range plans for the church there. He mapped out a four block by six block "area of influence" and developed a proposal for a community vegetable and flower garden, child care center, baby-sitters for mothers who attend health clinic, a preschool, and noonday meal for aged indigents. That was the short-range goal for a church of "not over 250 members." Long-range development, he proposed, would include a church-related camp, a home for the aged, and other outposts on the fringe of the area of influence as needed. All projects would be under pastor and church-council management with an advisory board.

Lark wrote, "The basic intent of the ministry of the church as it relates to the institutional programs of the entire plant should be to provide an opportunity for persons to get acquainted and establish a real working relationship with the Holy Spirit." The outreach ministry to find members for the body of Christ would be directed to hospitals, rest homes, jails, juvenile halls, drug addiction centers, regular home visitation, and general member canvassing. "The persons contacted," he wrote, "should be invited to become an active and working part of the body of Christ; then they should be given a job to do in the area of service they choose." The proposal had no takers. He had pinpointed the problems and proposed a program, changed the name of the church, had even bought a building lot for expansion, but the visionary tugboat found resistance in the conference. "Misunderstood in purpose, James Lark left Wichita a broken man," says Le Roy Bechler.

Lark's words remain and endure: "I feel that Spirit-filled personnel, a program adjusted to the spiritual needs of the community, and a plant suitable to carry out the program are essential in the building of a local church." The number of workers and the type of program and building will vary, he said, but not the aim. James Lark continuously kept the concern of ministry in the black community at the forefront of his efforts. "Is it building the black church?" he would ask. The larger church, Bechler believes, did not appreciate and realize the full potential of this man: "To some he was troublesome; others couldn't fully grasp what he was saying."

Gifted as a church planter perhaps more than as a pastor, Brother

Lark was innovative, creative, an organizer. He was full of ideas of what could be done and dared to believe it could be done. He had a deep love for the church and was hurt many times by unthinking responses of people. "He had a heavy burden for his people," Bechler says. "Many times he was frustated when words did not become actions in reaching people. Could it be that the low point in a period of his ministry may have been influenced in part by a vision too-tightly reined in?"

The Mennonite church that with a faith stronger than its culture had drawn the Larks in, had the capacity for including blacks, Lark said time and again. The old ship, though, seemed content to ply the familiar waters of the harbor, to the consternation, not without humor, of the "tugboater." James and Rowena Lark carried a vision of the church as a Spirit-directed community that excludes no one. It's a vision still tugging at the Mennonite Church. As the church in faith ventures out into the mission of Christ, people of every tribe, tongue, and race will be on board together. It just takes a few visionaries to lead the way.

James Henry Lark died on January 10, 1978. Rowena Lark preceded him in death on March 5, 1970. Their children are Dr. James Hill Lark, Austin, Texas; Mrs. Juanita Jewel Bell, Robbins, Illinois; Mrs. Essie Jean Lyons, Washington, D.C.; Mrs. Emma Waters, Chicago, Illinois; and Dr. Alexander Lark, Fresno, California.

The preface to James Lark's obituary is the well-known poem:

> One ship drives east and another drives west
> With the selfsame winds that blow.
> 'Tis the set of the sails and not the gales
> Which tells us the way to go.
> Like the winds of the sea are the ways of fate,
> As we voyage along through life:
> 'Tis the set of a soul
> That decides its goal,
> And not the calm or the strife.

The obituary ends with the verses from Ephesians 2:8-9, KJV: "For by grace are ye saved through faith; and that not of yourselves: it is the gift of God: not of works, lest any man should boast." Memorials were designated for the James H. Lark Scholarship Fund at Goshen College for development of black church leaders. The vision lives on.

5

THE ORIGINAL THIRTEEN MENNONITE CHURCH MISSIONS AMONG BLACKS, 1898-1950

For the Mennonite Church, mission work among the blacks, as already noted, began in the 1890s. Over the next half-century thirteen congregations emerged which in some manner or fashion reached out to the blacks. These developments are reviewed in this chapter.°

Pennsylvania
Welsh Mountain (1898). The beautiful Welsh Mountains are located in Lancaster County, Pennsylvania, and extend into an adjoining county to the east. These mountains separate two fertile valleys, both populated largely by Mennonite farmers.

In 1898 many of the black residents of the mountains were white with the exception of a black settlement in the Hand Boards area. A gang of white outlaws had made this area infamous years earlier, terrorizing blacks as well as white farmers living in the valley.

Through the efforts of the law, the threats and violence were largely reduced. Because of the subsistence economy of the area, however, a great deal of begging and stealing was done by the poor blacks, and this posed a constant annoyance to the people living in the valley.

One of the first home mission advocates for work in the Welsh Mountains area was John R. Buckwalter. He expressed his conviction

---

°While the main focus is on the missions established among blacks to 1950, brief updates on the congregations are included.

at the Lancaster Quarterly Meeting held on January 12, 1895. There he said, in part:

> We are in Lancaster City; we turn to the south and look over the beautiful Pequea Valley from the Susquehanna to the Chester County line. We turn to the north and look over the equally beautiful valley of the Conestoga, from Mount Joy to Morgantown, and what do we see? A powerful Mennonite Church strong in numbers and strong in means. We turn to the middle ground, or to the east, and we see among other scenes, the beautiful Welsh Mountains, peopled with a people to our certain knowledge of both races of whom it can be truly said as the Lord said of the Ninevites, that they cannot discern between the right hand and the left. And what have we as a church done to save them? PRACTICALLY NOTHING.

No immediate action resulted from Buckwalter's appeal. To keep the issue alive, however, persons in charge of the Mennonite Sunday School Mission meeting at Paradise, Pennsylvania, held July 1897, invited M. H. Hagler, a black Presbyterian minister, to speak. Pastor Hagler had for some years served in the Welsh Mountain area. He told of how in days past this wooded area offered a haven for many a slave who escaped into freedom. As the population grew, work became scarce causing poverty and lawlessness. He presented, in a convincing manner, the need for helping these people both physically and spiritually.

In response to Hagler's presentation, the Sunday School Mission took action to investigate mission opportunities in the mountains. They appointed a twelve-member board to assess the need. This investigation team discovered poverty firsthand. The cabins, shacks, and mud huts along with the filth, ignorance, and vice were appalling. As they observed the signs of social disorder—begging, stealing, drunkenness, and violence—they were convinced that the Welsh Mountain region was clearly a needy field ready for harvest.

The team, presenting their findings to the Sunday School Board proposed: "That we should rid the surrounding county of a very undesirable class of people inhabiting Welsh Mountain, not by driving them out, but by giving them a better condition spiritually by establishing Sunday schools and church services among them."

The board responded favorably, taking action to establish the Welsh Mountain Industrial Mission. They appointed Amos H.

Hershey and Samuel Musselman to open and supervise the work. They aimed to provide the blacks with work whereby they could earn an honest living.

On March 14, 1898, twenty-two men, along with a number of boys, reported for work. Their first job was to clear the land so that truck and farm crops could be planted. This project marked a new level of service and involvement for the Mennonite church in working with American blacks.

The following report published in the *New Era*, of Lancaster, Pennsylvania, describes the first year's work at Welsh Mountain Mission:

> A movement started some time since to make an organized effort to improve the moral and physical condition of the long neglected people on the Welsh Mountain has already been productive of much good and the prospects are very encouraging for a great amelioration of the blight that has for years dwelt upon that community and a general uplifting of its inhabitants in the not distant future. A number of the most prominent people in the county have enlisted with hearty zeal and intense interest in the work and below we publish the gratifying results that have attended their labors.
>
> At a meeting of the Mennonite Sunday School Mission held at Kinzer in January, 1898, a board of twelve directors was appointed with instruction to establish an Industrial Mission on Welsh Mountain, in the vicinity of the Hand Boards, with the object of giving employment to the neglected people living there, so as to give them a chance and by every honest means possible induce them to work for a living instead of begging and stealing. These people, on account of the many crimes they commit, entail a continuous expense on the county that must be met by taxation. Besides, they are a source of considerable expense and trouble and no little terror to the good people of the eastern end. With horses and wagons they scour the whole county, begging or stealing, and it is hoped by means of an Industrial Mission to educate and Christianize the rising generation so they may be useful citizens.
>
> What does the proposed Industrial Mission expect to do for them? First, buy some of the better sprout land on the mountain and have them clear it, then cultivate vegetables and fruits, for which the land is well adapted, raise broom corn and teach them to make brooms; teach the girls to wash and sew, be clean and decently dressed. All of the children's work at the mission will be paid for in the necessaries of life and as soon as they have become efficient and trustworthy the Directors will help them to positions for themselves. Sunday school and church services will be held regularly under the direction of Milton H. Hagler, an ordained colored minister.
>
> The success of the enterprise will depend on the aid given by a

charitable public and we cannot too eagerly urge the support of this splendid movement upon all citizens. In order to break up the begging habit, the people of the valleys will cease to feed the vagrants, but send them to the mission, where their wants can be provided for. The mission appeals for contributions of money, old clothing and shoes, old furniture, stoves and hardware. All of the following Directors will receive contributions, keep an account of the same, deliver the goods to the Mission, where they will be properly credited and an annual report made: S. H. Musselman, Chairman, Blue Ball; John R. Buckwalter, Vice Chairman, Ruyerstown; Noah Mack, Secretary, Farmersville; John Musselman, Treasurer, Intercourse; Jacob Mellings, Ronk's; Christian Neff, Strasburg; C. R. Herr, Lime Valley; Ephraim Hershey, Eby's; John A. Umble, Lime Valley; Benj. Weaver, Churchtown; B. F. Charles, East Petersburg; Harry Hershey, Intercourse.

Much progress has been made in the past year. Nine acres of timber land have been purchased by the Board and the colored people are now engaged in cutting cord wood, railroad ties, telephone poles, etc. The mission has also purchased a house situated on the road leading from the Hand Boards to Mt. Airy. Noah H. Mack and family will move there in the spring and take charge of the work. They will be accompanied by Miss Lydia Stauffer, who will assist in the work among the colored people. The colored children are attending the public schools fairly well, and crime has very materially decreased, as the Court record will show.

Bro. S. H. Musselman, who is the chairman of the Board, reports that to January 1, 1899, employment was given forty-three persons and the amount paid them in orders and provisions for labor was $893.90. The amount advanced beyond the earnings was $90.15 and $26.85 was expended charitably, making a total cost of $1,010.90. The highest amount earned by any one person was $110.85; the second highest, $90.78, and the third, $62.11. The above item of charity does not include the large amount of clothing, etc. that was distributed. The total offerings received for the year ending January 1, 1899, was $1,088.06. After the expenses were taken out the actual balance was $171.91.

S. H. Musselman, one of the men in charge, wrote to Noah Mack asking him to consider working in this needy field (as reported above). After consideration and prayer, Bro. and Sister Mack, with Lydia Stauffer, took charge of the mission.

With full-time workers, the Industrial Mission grew faster than the financial resources. Since the work was relatively new, however, it was felt that interest and support would grow throughout the church. The income from the mission, along with outside contributions, soon was sufficient to meet the financial needs.

Industry in the area emerged, too. In the fall of 1899, a structure was built to serve as a shirt, carpet-weaving, and broom factory. A mission home was built for the workers.

The workers set aside February 19, 1909, as a day of thanksgiving. The home bishop, Isaac Eby, delivered a sermon which was followed by a free meal served to eighty-five people from the community. This meeting was held in the new factory building. A joyous event also took place when Brother Mack and Pastor Hagler performed the marriage ceremonies of two couples from the community.

Even though Brother Mack was called into the ministry to serve the Groffdale-Metzler District on August 30, 1901, he did not accept immediately. He and his wife were determined to keep the mission open, and he also had to teach school to support his family. His wife and Lydia Stauffer spent much of their time working in the community store which they operated as part of the mission program. Brother Mack labored hard to keep the mission on its financial feet. In one of his pleas to the church for help (*Gospel Herald*, Jan. 13, 1910), he said, "Our situation is peculiar in that we are not recognized by any church or missionary body in the distribution of funds. We would beg you not to forget the crumbs in our behalf, or the real large 'fragments' as our standing debt amounts to several thousand dollars."

In the spring of 1910, Brother Mack moved to New Holland, Pennsylvania. He was succeeded by Levi Sauder and his wife, the former Lydia Stauffer. The Sauders' labors were cut short when they accepted the position of superintendent at the Millersville Orphanage. They left the following year.

One of the greatest difficulties besides finances was to secure workers, although many who had interest in the work gave as much time as they could. On April 1, 1913, Arthur T. Moyer came from Spring City, Pennsylvania, to help. Besides teaching in the public school, he served as mission superintendent.

As time went on, a gradual change took place at the mission. More time and attention was being given to the educational and spiritual welfare of the people. The building used for the shirt factory was converted into a comfortable schoolroom. The workers began a weekly Bible meeting class. Whenever a minister was available, a preaching service was held on Sunday evening. The workers believed that a more lasting work could be accomplished by seeking first the kingdom of God and making the educational and industrial part of the work dependent upon the spiritual.

On May 3, 1917, Elmer Boots, the first black member in Welsh Mountain, was baptized by Bishop C. M. Brackbill.

John F. Bressler conducted the first revival meetings in February 1920. Among the visible results were six confessions of faith.

On January 24, 1924, the mission was saddened when Brother Moyer was shot and seriously wounded by a resident of the community who was stealing corn from a barn near the schoolhouse. Moyer died a week later without naming the thief. However the person was apprehended anyway and given a long prison sentence. Following Moyer's death, sister Emma Rudy of Lancaster, Pennsylvania, was appointed as a worker. J. Paul and Phebe (Martin) Graybill, who were serving the mission in Philadelphia, came to assist in the work. Brother Graybill finished the unexpired term of Brother Moyer as teacher in the public school. They remained for the spring and summer, after which they returned to Philadelphia to resume the charge there. In 1926 Emma Rudy was asked to carry out her call to the full-time Christian service in Philadelphia. She continued there until she retired in 1961.

By the mid-twenties, the industrial part of the mission had seemingly fulfilled its purpose. People in the community were beginning to take hold of their destiny and were becoming self-sufficient. They were finding employment elsewhere. The workers believed energies should now be invested in establishing an old people's home. The Samaritan Home in a beautiful mountain setting resulted. In October 1924, the mission's name was changed to the Welsh Mountain Mission and Samaritan Home. Brother Benjamin Buckwalter assumed direction of this work. (The response was so great that by 1950 the home had been enlarged twice to a total capacity of 50—but up to that date none of the residents had been black.)

The Mennonite work in Welsh Mountain began with the understanding that the spiritual needs of the people would be met by their own existing churches. Through the years, Mennonites offered a limited amount of supportive spiritual ministry, but at the time of the decline of the Industrial Mission, the local black pastor was growing older and more inactive. With this turn of events, the mission began to assume more spiritual responsibility. With increased staff involvement in the operation of the Samaritan Home, however, less time and efforts were made to minister to the blacks. This continued until 1938 when a request was presented to Lancaster Conference for assistance in ministering to the black community. The conference responded by appointing Ira Buckwalter as superintendent. In 1982 Mark M. Leaman served as bishop and Clayton D. Leaman and Ira D. Buckwalter as ministers.

Under Buckwalter's leadership a new effort was made to reach the black community. Records indicate that the Sunday attendance of blacks between 1938 and 1950 averaged around 40, but then, beginning in the fifties and on into the sixties, a decline set in. In 1982 the membership stood at 61.

What conclusions may be drawn from this experience of working in a black community for more than three-quarters of a century? Although the original intention was to establish a church and to meet a spiritual need, no solid church has ever emerged. The industrial phase appears to have been the dominant emphasis. Workers expended much effort and sacrifice; one worker lost his life. The pioneers of this first Mennonite mission among blacks saw a need and urged the church to become involved. Maybe their zeal was greater than their knowledge of what the implications might be in beginning a cross-cultural ministry.

When the industrial phase of this witness ended, to meet another need the church established a retirement home. The irony of the situation is that blacks were never admitted into the home. White Mennonites still regarded blacks condescendingly, as making up another class of people. In those early years when several elderly blacks needed care, a sister of the church took one woman into her home and cared for her until she died. She later took in another. In 1938 a new effort was made to reach the blacks in the community.

The discriminating practices of the old people's home, as well as frequent leadership changes, a predominately white leadership, rigid church discipline, and a projection of white cultural patterns of lifestyle and worship, probably contributed to the mission's demise.

It should be noted that the long-term efforts of the mission did have a significant impact upon the people who received help. Probably the greatest benefit, however, was received by those who felt called to minister to a needy and deprived people. This was an outlet to help those in need. The motives, without doubt, were pure. The goals, however, were not clear; nor was the future and the end result. A vision for providing a significant witness in the black community had yet to emerge.

Lancaster Colored Mission (1933), renamed South Christian Street Mennonite Church (1939). What was to become the second mission outreach in the black community (the Lancaster Colored Mission, later called South Christian Street Mennonite Church) emerged indirectly 35 years after Welsh Mountain Mission, in Lancaster, Pennsylvania.

There were already several Mennonite churches in the city of Lancaster, one established as long before as 1824. In the early 1930s, Elam Stauffer conducted a series of revival meetings at the Rawlinsville Mennonite Church. During these meetings, five Jones children from a black family accepted Christ as their Savior. Following these meetings, the question arose about a church home for the black converts. The very fact that this question surfaced indicated that the church had a problem in its attitude toward blacks. This attitude reflected white society's opposition to racial mixing.

What would be the result if the church allowed the races to mix? Should the church blaze new trails in social relations or should the church consider only the best way to reach the black community apart from social interaction? The Rawlinsville Mennonite Church faced two options. They could either organize a mission for blacks, or they could encourage blacks to worship with one of the existing Mennonite congregations. The latter was already happening at the Vine Street Mission. To resolve the issue, representatives from the Rawlinsville and Vine Street churches contacted the Eastern Mennonite Board of Missions and Charities about the problem. The Eastern Board authorized the formation of a new, separate church for blacks in the city of Lancaster.

Following an investigation for a location and leadership, a room was rented at 317 Howard Avenue. J. S. Lehman from the Vine Street Mission was appointed superintendent. On November 5, 1933, with six teachers and 22 Sunday school pupils present, the work began. Bishop D. Stoner Krady brought the message.

The Jones children, who were converts at Rawlinsville, were

brought over to this mission each Sunday. After receiving proper instruction they were all baptized into the church on December 10, 1933, by bishop John H. Mosemann.

The mission grew as workers engaged in active work among the blacks. Growth helped engender enthusiasm, and soon the average attendance had reached 60—overextending the available classroom space. To teach effectively, the mission needed adequate facilities. Upon advice from the sponsoring Eastern Board, the workers looked for a larger place. The Lord answered their prayers by providing a rental dwelling at 460 Rockland Street. The workers lived in the rear of the building while the main part, a room 18 by 27 feet, was used as an auditorium and a place for Sunday school. The first service in the new location was held on July 1, 1934.

Once a congregation was established, the need arose for a pastor to carry on the work more effectively. On March 31, 1935, Brother J. S. Lehman was voted to this position and was immediately ordained to take charge.

With a strong visitation program, the work steadily increased. By January 1936, the mission had a membership of ten. The attendance had grown to over eighty. Again there was the problem of seating and classroom space. Eastern Board gave assurance that as soon as possible a new church building would be provided, but this problem was not taken care of until 1938 when the board took action to build. At that time, the average attendance was 104.

The conference and congregation built a brick facility at the corner of South Christian and Locust streets. This provided adequate classrooms and a seating capacity for 300—truly an answer to prayer. The dedicatory service was held on February 19, 1939.

With a new church building, the work continued to grow; attendance soon averaged 144. On October 5, 1945, twenty-six members participated in a communion service and observed the ordinance of foot washing.

As the work load increased, the need developed for someone to assist Brother Lehman in his pastoral work. Bishop D. Stoner Krady secured permission from the Lancaster Conference to ordain a deacon. On August 15, 1946, Andrew Landis was chosen by lot to take up the position.

The mission suffered a significant loss when Brother Landis was killed in an accident on March 25, 1948. To fill the gap, Lester Weaver, who was then serving as Sunday school superintendent, was chosen by lot and ordained on August 15, 1948.

From its founding until 1949 the mission was faithfully supplied with Sunday school and Bible school teachers by surrounding churches. With the help of these teachers, a well-planned visitation program was carried on. This home visitation program was probably the greatest single factor in the growth of the mission. Prior to 1950 no denomination in the community had conducted a summer Bible school. There was a positive response to the Mennonite efforts.

During that period friends sent in supplies such as vegetables and canned fruit. These made it possible to give needy families a Christmas basket.

Four all-day meetings were held each year. Two of these days were set apart for fasting and prayer; the other two were for inspirational meetings. During the summer months, street meetings were held instead of cottage prayer meetings.

In the fall of 1949, several sisters who were interested in the young people started a sewing class for the girls and also some activities for the boys. During the nineteen-fifties and sixties, many of the whites who served as workers continued to worship with the congregation as members.

The city's Urban Renewal Program produced a population shift when old single dwellings were razed and apartment buildings were built. This move had an adverse effect on black attendance.

In the late nineteen-seventies, Pastor Lester Weaver turned the reins of leadership over to James R. Garman. Since then, the membership has sustained a balance of various ethnic groups, although the desired black leadership has never materialized. Currently, Nelson H. Lehman serves as minister. Membership in 1986 was 60.

Diamond Street Mennonite Church (1935). The mission outreach to blacks in Philadelphia began 35 years after Mennonites started doing mission work in that city. Mennonites had settled in Philadelphia in the latter part of the seventeenth century. While a Mennonite congregation has existed continuously since then in Germantown, the Mennonites found their way to the rich soil of the surrounding rural areas as the city grew. They came to the city to shop and market their goods. A number of persons, including Isaac Kulp, a weekly market vendor from Bucks County, developed a conviction to establish a Christian witness in the city.

At the turn of the twentieth century about forty Mennonites lived in Philadelphia. With the support of Franconia Conference Mennonites who lived in the city, and from the Lancaster Sunday School Mission (forerunner of Eastern Mennonite Board of Missions and Charities), the Philadelphia Mennonite Mission opened in 1899 at 1930 East Howard Street. John Mellinger, Isaac Kulp, and Joseph Bechtold had selected the location.

The work was conducted along the lines of the Mennonite Chicago Home Mission with Sunday school, sewing school, children's meetings, and preaching (when a preacher was supplied). Daniel Kauffman, the Mennonite statesman and writer, preached the first sermon in July 1899. Two Lancaster women, Mary Denlinger and Amanda Musselman, were called to Philadelphia from the Chicago Home Mission and were the stabilizing force as the mission grew. Almost 25 years elapsed before a resident pastor was assigned to the mission to develop a congregation.

The Philadelphia Mennonite Mission relocated to an empty store at Dauphin and Amber streets when it outgrew the first facility. In 1907 it was moved to a more permanent home at 2151 East Howard Street in the same area. This mission, in a then predominately white area, grew into the Norris Square Mennonite Church, located slightly east of the center of the city. Today it is the Arca de Salvación Mennonite congregation at 2147 N. Howard Street.

As was true in many northern industrial cities, Philadelphia from the 1930s into the 1950s experienced an influx of labor from the south. Factories needed workers. Blacks, looking for new opportunities, came north en masse. In the early thirties a large number of blacks moved to Philadelphia and a few started attending the Mennonite mission on Howard Street.

The large influx of new settlers sparked racial tension and conflict. How was the little Mennonite mission to respond to this new phenomenon? Workers at the Norris Square congregation developed an interest in reaching out to the black families who had settled in the vicinity of the mission. Summer Bible school, started in 1926, provided such an opportunity. After nine years of summer Bible school work, black children made up one-fourth of the total attendance. The *Diamond Street Congregational History* (1950) records:

> Because of various problems which have arisen it has been felt wise to have the colored and white children in separate schools. In the summer of 1934 the two schools were separate for the first time; but both were in buildings in connection with the mission.

In 1935 the mission workers rented a building at 191 West Dauphin Street a few blocks from the Norris Square congregation. The "Mennonite Mission for Colored," so named at the suggestion of James Lark, opened there on July 1.

Emma Rudy and later Alma Ruth were the mission workers, assisted by Mennonite students, Norris Square members, and visiting ministers. The mission emphasized teaching and preaching the Word. J. Paul Graybill, who had been sent by the Lancaster Mission in 1922 to the Philadelphia mission, held preaching and superintendent responsibility at the outset. He was assisted in the pulpit for shorter periods by Merle Eshleman and Noah H. Mack. At first no Sunday school was held, but each Sunday evening featured a children's meeting followed by a sermon. In 1927 Graybill helped set up a large summer Bible school, a first among the sponsoring groups.

Graybill left Philadelphia at the end of 1939 to become bishop of the Weaverland district of Lancaster Conference. G. Irvin Lehman became superintendent, followed in June 1940 by John H. Mosemann, a missionary on furlough from Africa. Clarence Fretz took over as superintendent and preacher at the end of 1940 and continued for about one year.

The work grew steadily despite frequent changes in leadership. By 1940 the prospects for attendance were so high that no summer or winter Bible school was held. The same was true the following year. Attention now shifted to include ministry with adults. Emma Rudy and Alma Ruth began visitation in homes and hospitals, cottage meetings, street meetings, women's sewing circle, and home Bible studies.

"The sowing of the seed on Dauphin Street was not without a harvest," writes Robert W. Good in an unpublished paper on the Diamond Street congregation (1982). In 1936 an elderly man, Charles Mills, began attending services. On September 27, 1936, he stood during a testimony period and asked to become a member of the church.

"J. Paul Graybill who would officiate his baptism," Good writes, "was unexpectedly called to Florida. While he was gone Charles Mills took sick with the flu, suffered a stroke, and died on January 19, 1937, never receiving the right hand of fellowship in the Mennonite church."

On November 27, 1938, Alleanor Jenkins and her two daughters, Edna and Grace, were received as the first black members of the Mennonite mission. When these women a little over a month earlier had begun to wear plain clothes, Emma Rudy wrote in her diary: "This marks the happy experience of seeing our first applicants wearing the plain clothes, and more than that is seeing them come out victoriously for the Lord."

In 1941 the mission secured a new location 20 blocks away at 1814 West Diamond Street. Clinton Ferster was appointed superintendent. Few from the Dauphin Street group attended in the new location.

Brother J. Harold Brenneman became the first ordained pastor. Several times the progress of the mission suffered due to a lack of workers. The mission was able, however, to continue holding Bible schools each summer with attendance over 100. Street meetings were conducted each week as workers were available. Regular Sunday worship children's meetings, and prayer services were also held.

Membership growth came slowly. The congregation had four black members in 1950. It seemed difficult to reach the youth. Pastor Brenneman, who continued at the mission until the fall of 1950, summed up the problems and needs this way:

> We are living among the working class of Negroes. There is a form of godliness, but many deny the power thereof in their lives. There is a terrible ignorance of the Scriptures even by many who are church members. Many resent the continual plea of pastors for money. I feel that many are hungering for the truth and really want to know. I believe the time is ripe for the Mennonite church with her emphasis on faith and practice to enter the field more largely.
>
> The laborers for this harvest are few. Non-resident Sunday school teachers and workers present a problem. The changing of Sunday school teachers which is frequent has been a matter that continues to require an answer.

Robert W. Good writes that between 1942 and 1946, "a neon sign appeared on the front of 1814 West Diamond with an invitation:

'Come to Jesus.' Thereby the mission became known in the community as the 'Come to Jesus Church.' " He observes further: "Slowly, people were attracted both to Jesus and to the services the mission offered. With only three members the little mission had proved many times it could involve capacity numbers in its programs."

J. Paul Graybill suggested three reasons why the mission had not grown more since its beginning: the complex life in an old city, the social differences between races, and the lack of permanent workers in the first years. He believed a united effort on the part of the church in Bible teaching, in prayer, and in providing balanced social activities for the blacks would result in progress.

Since then, the congregation has taken on both new life and vision. Luke and Miriam Stoltzfus came in the summer of 1951. They were instrumental in the transition from mission to church. They changed the name to Diamond Street Mennonite Church, and also the checking account, which had read, African Mennonite Church. In 1978 the congregation adopted a new organizational structure which involves more of the membership in leadership roles. Its vision was enlarged when it purchased a former Masonic Temple at 1632 West Diamond Street for $1.00. A million dollar renovation of this large structure into a place for various types of community ministries as well as for a worship center for the congregation has been in process for several years.

Currently, Freeman Miller, a white, serves as pastor and Charles Baynard, Sr., a black, serves as associate. In 1986 the membership at Diamond Street was 101.

Andrew's Bridge (1938). In a rural community in southern Lancaster County near Christiana, Pennsylvania, emerged the Andrew's Bridge Fellowship. This community became the home of many slaves who had escaped to find freedom. A Presbyterian Church that had split off from another church on the issue of slavery offered the former slaves a place where they could worship. At the close of the Civil War, however, the interest of the membership waned and finally the church closed its doors.

In the mid-thirties, members of surrounding Mennonite churches became interested in this community. A survey revealed that a significant number of both whites and blacks had no direct church affiliation and that there was a desire on the part of local people to begin a Sunday school. The Thompson home in the community opened its doors for the first service on January 8, 1938, with 21 in attendance. Every two weeks, for seven years, services were held in the Thompson home.

When efforts were made to find more adequate facilities, the lot where a vacant church had been torn down was given free of charge to the Eastern Mennonite Board of Missions. Plans were immediately made to build, and four months later, on December 9, 1945, the dedication of the new building took place.

At a series of revivals which followed, seven people made profession of faith. Shortly thereafter, the members organized with a charter membership of 30. Brother Jacob Mellinger was chosen by lot and ordained as pastor on June 5, 1946. The membership in 1950 was 50, of which ten were black.

Andrew's Bridge Fellowship experienced what many other rural communities went through; many of their younger people moved to the cities. The church growth has been small, and gradually the number of blacks has declined. In 1986 the membership was 63 and predominately white. Blacks have not held significant offices within the local congregation, but several are involved in other Mennonite churches. Edwin H. Ranck, ordained in 1965, is pastor. Other ministers are Ephraim Nafziger and Phares O. Lantz.

Seventh Street Mission (1938), renamed Buttonwood Mennonite Fellowship (1971). The Seventh Street Mission was planted in the industrial city of Reading, Pennsylvania, on January 8, 1922. The city is of historical importance since it was laid out by the William Penn family. Located in a coal mining region, it was the home of over 500 manufacturing plants, including the largest silk stocking factory in the world.

Members of the Mennonite churches near the city became interested in establishing a witness in Reading. In cooperation with the Eastern Mennonite Board of Missions, investigations were made which resulted in the beginning of a Sunday school there in 1922.

As an industrial center, Reading attracted blacks from the south. Many of those living near the mission began attending the services.

Friction developed over the advisibility of the races mixing. This led to the establishment of a separate Reading mission for the blacks.

In 1938 a rented house on Neversink Street was renovated and equipped to serve as a worship center. Sunday school was held regularly, and preaching services were frequent. Evangelistic meetings were held once a year.

Several years later, the Mission Board purchased a building at 347 South Seventh Street.

The leaders found the work difficult. Brother N. G. Good reported that the blacks did not respond as readily to Mennonite principles and doctrines as one might hope. He wrote, "They are slow to accept because they have not had the background to understand the prayer head covering, plain garb, positions on movies and insurance. Young men under instruction withdrew on account of our attitude towards employment in war industries and accepting military service."

This difficulty affected the mission's outreach into the community. In 1950 the mission reported no members other than the workers.

During the fifties and sixties the mission began ministering primarily to the whites in the community. Though a number of blacks were attending the services, many began to move because of poor housing into a northern part of the city known as the Buttonwood community.

In 1970-71 the pastor, William Weaver, was successful in leading the church to purchase a store front building in the Buttonwood area which was renovated for services. Out of this extension from Seventh Street, Samuel Brown united with the church and later was chosen to serve as pastor at Buttonwood. Ertell Whigham also became part of the leadership, but later he moved to Philadelphia where he is a minister in the Diamond Street Mennonite Church. In 1986 Paul Angstadt, Jr., served as pastor. The congregation had 17 members.

Virginia

Broad Street Mennonite Mission (1935). The Broad Street witness began as the first Mennonite Church black mission established south of the Mason-Dixon line. It was located in the northeastern section of Harrisonburg, Virginia, the conference seat of the Mennonites in Virginia, as well as the home of Eastern Mennonite High School, College, and Seminary.

The historical development of this mission dramatizes both the successes and the failures experienced by sincere people who tried to fulfill their role as God's people by sharing the gospel of Jesus Christ.

"The History of Broad Street Mennonite Church, 1936-1971," a paper written by John Weber, gives an excellent account of the historical events and struggles during this period. He reports that a young woman named Thelma McConnell, an Eastern Mennonite School student, out of a heart of love and concern for the blacks, began to visit the "Negro section" of Harrisonburg on Sunday afternoons in the early 1930s. She witnessed to blacks in their homes and on the streets. This opened the way for the Young People's Christian Association (YPCA) of Eastern Mennonite College to become involved in establishing a witness.

The YPCA began to visit in both black and white homes, holding "cottage prayer meetings." The response was so favorable and so successful that the students asked the Virginia Mennonite Board of Missions and Charities for assistance. Although the board investigated the situation (1935-36), nothing was done until the students of the YPCA took the initiative, found a building at the corner of Gay and Federal Streets, and paid the first month's rent.

The first Sunday school began in June of 1936 with the whites meeting in the morning, and the blacks in the afternoon. This arrangement was in keeping with the tradition of separate worship for the races. Sunday night preaching services were held alternately for each group. No immediate effort was made to baptize or receive members into the church. After several months, the dual use of the building was discontinued when the whites moved to the Chicago Avenue location.

Ernest G. Gehman served as director of the mission and YPCA activities. In September 1938 Ernest Swartzentruber was appointed superintendent, and in October the worship services were shifted to the mornings.

The success of the YPCA workers was soon evident from the response of the children in the community. YPCA emphasis on home visitation and friendly relationships began to nurture trust and confidence. These students were sincere and sensed a duty to share their love. They saw the city as a place to carry out the great commission. They were there to *do* mission work.

That same year a controversy emerged over the issue of inviting blacks into church membership. It was debated whether or not evangelistic meetings should even be held for fear of converts. As the debate progressed, the suggestion was made to close the mission if the workers couldn't invite people to Christ and to church membership. Ernest Swartzentruber concurred, if they couldn't do evangelistic work, they should "close the mission and stop playing church."

The mission was not closed, however, and within the year evangelistic meetings were held. It was not until several years later, on December 1, 1940, that four blacks were officially received as members. The foundation for this event had been laid in the work of Mrs. Rowena Lark from Washington, D.C. Several years earlier, she had come to help "in the invitation work." The workers had thought she would be an asset in the visitation programs by persuading community people to come to the mission.

The first communion service was held on March 16, 1941. However, to the dismay of the workers, the communion was held separately for blacks and whites.

In November 1940, the executive committees of the Virginia Mennonite Conference and the Virginia Mennonite Mission Board had formulated a working policy for the two races. Conference accepted the action during its annual session in August 1941. The 1940 policy document said:

Policy Governing the Organization
of a Mennonite Colored Organization

At a joint meeting of the Executive Committee of the Virginia Mennonite Conference and the Executive Committee of the Virginia Mennonite Board of Missions and Charities held at the home of Etter F. Heatwole, November 11, 1940, Bishop S. H. Rhodes presented the matter of fixing definite policies to govern relationships between the colored and white in Mennonite church fellowship. A motion was passed adopting the following recommendations as an official statement of our policy:

In view of the general attitude of society in the South toward the intermingling of the two races and inasmuch as we desire to adopt a practical working policy with the view of promoting the best interests for both colored and white, and since as a matter of expediency we must

•

make some distinction to meet existing conditions, we propose the following course of procedure in establishing a Mennonite colored congregation.

1. *Aim*—It is our aim to build up a colored congregation under a separate but auxiliary organization of the Virginia Mennonite Conference.

2. *Baptism*—We recommend that the bishop in charge proceed with the administration of the ordinance of baptism in the usual manner and after extending the right hand of fellowship, the applicant should be greeted by a colored brother or colored sister.

3. *Salutation and Feetwashing*—Keeping in line with our present practice of making a distinction between the sexes in the observance of feetwashing and of the kiss of charity, we do not recommend the practice of these two ordinances between white and colored.

4. *Communion*—We recommend that provision be made for the use of individual cups at the communion table and that participation in the communion be restricted to the colored and those who are regular workers among them.

(Minutes, Executive Committee, Virginia Mennonite Mission Board, 1931-1947).

Grace Showalter, librarian of Menno Simons Historical Library/ Archives at Eastern Mennonite College, supplied the text of the 1940 *Policy*. She said, "I always have mixed feelings about discussions of that earlier era. While it is true that the Southern position was wrong, there is a sense in which paragraph two of the 1940 *Policy* statement does reflect a bit of the dilemma of Southern Mennonites in trying to fit into the prevailing social ethic and yet do what they knew was right in relating to and in reaching nonchurched blacks. It is true that we did reflect the social mores of the South where we had lived for over 150 years, but, in that period, confrontation as a way of combating society's ills was not a tactic of the Mennonite Church anywhere."

These policies were immediately challenged by Ernest Swartzentruber, but to little avail. Some in the church were ready to abide by these policies, while others only accepted them to keep peace. Others refused to accept the restrictive policy at all, notably Ernest Swartzentruber, who resigned his position as mission superintendent.

In 1942, after requests for more permanent facilities, the Mission Board purchased land on the corner of Broad and Effinger Streets. It was not until April 1945 that actual construction began. By October the building was completed enough to hold its first services. The name was then changed from the Gay Street Mission to the Broad Street Mission.

During the late forties and into the fifties, strong visitation programs and various types of interest programs were used to reach the people. One of the active members was Mrs. Roberta Webb, 96 years old in 1985. In 1966 she was the first black to become a resident of Virginia Mennonite Home. "Sister Webb," wrote congregational historian Harold E. Huber, "is a constant joy and inspiration, a warmhearted Christian. She absorbed the racial problems with true Christian love." Sister Webb taught elementary school in Harrisonburg for many years. Another much-loved couple, now deceased, David (Uncle Pete) and Vada (Aunt Vada) Cubbage, joined the church in 1945.

By 1950 a total of 27 blacks had become members. In 1954 the membership was 24 and it continued to decline thereafter.

A number of changes caused this decline. Some of these were related to race, some to a philosophy of missions approach, and some to the important fact that white attendance had increased. One of the earlier pastors, Ralph Shank, had warned in the conference publication that if too many visitors came to the mission, the Negro people would not come (*Missionary Light*, 1954).

The mission did make efforts in the early fifties to become involved in social issues. In July 1955, a year after the Supreme Court struck down the "separate but equal policy," an action was taken by the Virginia Conference to rescind their 1941 policy on racial separation. "There has been progress in attitudes of our own people towards the New Testament principles in matters of race relations" (*Missionary Light*, 1955). This action was, in effect, an apology for the previous policy.

The complexion of the membership, which had begun to change in the fifties, continued changing through the seventies. White attendance increased; black attendance decreased.

The influx of white members brought about a change in church structure and organization. The community people of the past never had ownership, even though (Billy) Curry was ordained as deacon in October 1961. This was the first congregational office held by a black up to this time. Another black member, Arnold Hackney, was actively involved as a song leader. During 1968-70 Pastor John Ehst, a white student at EMC, learned to know many community youths through recreation activities. George Richards, a young black from Baltimore, served as pastoral assistant 1970-71 while studying at EMC.

Richard Weaver was pastor from 1957 to 1978 (with a two-year absence in the middle of the period). From 1970 until the fall of 1978, when Richard retired, the congregation was mostly young persons, including many college students. Charismatic worship and ministry were emphasized.

Beginning in 1978, the congregation took a new direction. That fall the group chose a four-person ministry team which began to lead in the development of a different approach to church life and mission, emphasizing relationships and reconciliation. One of the three major congregational goals now is relating and ministering to the people—black and white—of Harrisonburg's northeast community. In 1986 the pastoral team of "enablers" included Harold E. Huber, Ken Handrich, Vida Huber, and John Jantzi. The congregation had 42 members.

California

Thirty-fifth Street Mennonite Mission (1940). The first Mennonite church in Los Angeles, California, was officially organized in the early twenties. Members built a meetinghouse at 151 West 73rd Street. In the late thirties, the congregation organized a craft program for children and a number of black children attended.

Interest in work with blacks developed, and the congregation made plans to start a program for black children at a facility on 35th Street. When no one showed up for the first meeting, the workers offered each boy who would come a nickel if he would bring another. The inducement worked, and interest increased.

The first Sunday school met in November 1940 with three pupils. Several Sundays after that no one came. Undaunted, the workers kept on, and soon attendance reached 65. Several years later seven participants became members.

In 1948 membership reached an all time high of 13, but by 1950 only five members remained.

Harry E. Shoup was chosen from the Calvary congregation to

serve as superintendent. Workers were furnished by the congregation and members of Voluntary Service units were involved in the summers. The mission closed in the mid-fifties.

Illinois

Bethel Mennonite Church (1944). It was not until the early forties that the first Midwestern ministry of Mennonites to the black community emerged in Chicago, the second largest urban center in America.

In 1893 Mennonite workers had opened the first urban home missions witness in Chicago. This was followed by a Spanish witness in 1933. In 1943-44 the pastors, Raymond Yoder and Lester T. Hershey, had a concern for a witness in the black community. After exploring the field, a group of Goshen College students responded to an appeal to conduct a survey in one of the large government housing projects.

The students found a positive response to the idea of a Christian witness, and they made immediate plans to have a summer Bible school. Efforts were also made to secure teachers, including a call to a black couple, James and Rowena Lark, from Quakertown, Pennsylvania, to serve as superintendents. The Larks agreed to come and conduct a two-week Bible school, August 21 to September 2, 1944. The school was so successful that the children were invited to return the following Sunday afternoon when the first Sunday school was held on September 3, 1944, in the Douglass Center building on the corner of Loomis and 14th Place. This was followed by the first prayer meeting on September 5, 1944, in the nearby Tunstall home.

The Larks, after completing the Bible school, helped organize the beginning of the church before returning to their home in Pennsylvania. The governing board for the mission included William Brenneman, Theodore Wentland, and Walter Yordy. William Brenneman was appointed pastor and Walter Yordy superintendent. The board soon felt the need for a regular worker. They extended a call to the Larks to come back to Chicago to assume leadership of the church. The Larks accepted the invitation, and in the latter part of February 1945, James, Rowena, and their five children arrived.

The meeting place was moved to a building at 14th Place and Loomis that was leased for five years. This gave the mission a more

Summer Bible school at Bethel Mennonite Mission, Chicago, Illinois, in 1946. James and Rowena Lark were pastor and superintendent.

James and Rowena Lark barbecuing ribs with Mary Alice Shaum and Alta Byler at Camp Rehoboth, St. Anne, Illinois, in 1949.

Rowena and James Lark with son, Alexander, in front of their Chicago home in 1947.

Voluntary Service unit Rosalie Garber, Florence
Weaver, Merle Bender, and Le Roy Bechler,
Chicago, 1947.

Le Roy Bechler with Bible school class at Bethel Mennonite Church, Chicago, 1947.

Housing at Camp Ebenezer, Holmes County, Ohio, 1947.

Le Roy Bechler, Ramon Tang, and
an unidentified boy from Chicago at
Camp Ebenezer in 1947.

Camp Ebenezer staff, Holmes County, Ohio, 1947.

Bible class at
Camp Ebenezer,
1947.

Le Roy Bechler with four junior-age boys from Chicago at Camp Ebenezer, 1947.

Enjoying the swimming hole at Camp Ebenezer, Holmes County, Ohio, 1948.

Le Roy Bechler leading chapel at Camp Ebenezer, 1948.

Mealtime at Camp Ebenezer, 1948. Adults (left to right) are Elsie Burckhart, Tillie Yoder, Ruby Oaks, Le Roy Bechler, and Ada Webb.

Irene and Le Roy Bechler (left) entertaining the young married group at Saginaw, Michigan, 1954, including John Wicker (center) and Velma Hall (right). Floyd Hall took the picture.

VS unit housing for the first summer Bible school effort at Saginaw, Michigan, in 1949.

The lower grades of the Ninth Street Mennonite Church summer Bible school in 1952 or 1953, meeting in the nearby Hispanic church.

Summer Bible school teaching staff, made up of Voluntary Service persons and members of Ninth Street Mennonite Church, Saginaw, Michigan.

A group from Ninth Street Mennonite Church, Saginaw, Michigan, on a visit to Gladstone Mennonite Church, Cleveland, Ohio, in 1952.

Le Roy Bechler with Donald Holdern and Eugene Moten at a camp on Raymond Byler's farm, Pigeon, Michigan, 1952.

Summer Bible school participants at Ninth Street Mennonite Church, Saginaw, Michigan, in 1955 or 1956.

Youth group with church bus at Ninth Street Mennonite Church, Saginaw, Michigan, 1955.

Several summer Bible school classes at Ninth Street Mennonite Church in 1955.

Rowena Lark (back right) meeting with the WMSC at the Ninth Street Mennonite Church parsonage in 1954. Others (left to right): Irene Bechler, Corrine Taylor, Willa Mae Wicker, Inez Patilla, Ruby Wicker, and Rosalie Arthur.

James and Rowena Lark, 1951.

Youth sponsor Grace Sparks, James H. Lark, and Pastor Le Roy Bechler just before the dedication of Harmony House Day Care and Youth Center, Saginaw, Michigan, 1956.

The extension Sunday school at Carrollton, Michigan, 1956, sponsored by Ninth Street Mennonite Church, Saginaw, Michigan.

Le Roy Bechler (right) with the Finance Committee of Ninth Street Mennonite Church (left to right): John Wicker, Willa Mae Wicker, and Floyd Hall. They are standing in front of the newly purchased and remodeled Harmony House Day Care and Youth Center.

The registration table at the convention for black youth from Chicago, Cleveland, Saginaw, and Youngstown—held at the Yellow Creek Mennonite Church, Goshen, Indiana, 1959.

permanent base of operation. The Larks very early sensed that juvenile delinquency was a major community problem. Gang members, ages 7 to 17, became the major focus of their ministry. The Larks began to provide such activities as a girls sewing club and a club for the boys. Through this concentrated effort, the effects began to be felt in the community. Gangs were broken up. Parents cooperated. As a result, the church services drew more people and thus broadened the spiritual ministry in the community.

On December 2, 1945, the Chicago workers opened an extension Sunday school in the Dearborn Street area. This became known as the Dearborn Street Mission. Services were held on Sunday afternoons to enable the Larks and workers from Bethel to provide leadership. The Dearborn effort closed in the fifties when workers and finances were not available to enable the ministry to develop further.

In the summer of 1946 contact was made between Pastor Lark and a Mennonite farm family near Millersburg, Ohio, who had a large vacant house on their farm. Brother Lark envisioned starting a camp for the boys and girls in the inner city. The Yoders opened the door for this to happen, and a group of boys accompanied by a counselor were sent to Ohio for two weeks. This experience gave birth to the summer camping program for city children. Children from both Cleveland and Youngstown came. Camp Luz, currently owned by the Ohio Mennonite Conference, is the outgrowth of the camp on the farm.

The distance of sending children to Ohio and Brother Lark's own vision led him to purchase ten acres of woodland near St. Anne, Illinois, 60 miles south of Chicago. This camping site for the children from Bethel became Camp Rehoboth.

It soon became evident that more adequate church facilities were needed for Bethel. Mennonite Board of Missions, which sponsored the work in Chicago, arranged for the Larks to visit churches throughout the United States to solicit funds for a new building. The Larks raised $114,000. On September 26, 1954, Bethel's newly built facility was dedicated. In the morning service Brother Lark was ordained as the first black bishop in the Mennonite Church. Eight years earlier, Brother Lark had been the first ordained black minister in the church.

The following year, 1955, Paul and Lois King joined the pastoral staff to help minister to the approximately 800 new families that were moving into the housing area around Bethel. Plans were made to set up a day-care center. By 1956 it began operation.

Through 1961, Bethel's attendance continued to increase, with over 212 enrolled in Sunday school, and an average worship attendance of 180. Easter attendance that year reached 400.

As club interest grew, a need for a more structured club program for boys and girls became apparent. This concern was felt by other inner city churches also. Workers in the black missions developed the Wayfarer's Club materials which were later released by Mennonite Publishing House.

Bishop Lark had a deep concern for boys and girls and through his vision over 500 attended summer Bible schools.

Paul O. King became pastor at Bethel when the Larks gave their attention to beginning a mission in the Camp Rehoboth community. Bishop Lark continued to oversee the work at Bethel. In 1956 the Larks moved to St. Louis to plant a new congregation there. This became the Bethesda Mennonite Church. Hubert and June Schwartzentruber assumed responsibility for the Bethesda work in November 1957. Leamon Sowell later served as pastor. In 1950 the membership at Bethel was 52. In 1986 membership stood at 62.

Some questions deserve reflection: Why were so few blacks assimilated into the membership and life of the church at Bethel during its zenith when there were new facilities, large attendance, and a great potential for growth? Though the momentum continued high when white leadership replaced the Larks, why did a later decline in attendance occur? Was the civil rights struggle of the sixties a factor? Even under black leadership, it appears that Bethel has not recaptured the level of vitality it achieved in the fifties and early sixties.

Dearborn Street Mission (1945). At the request of a community family to James Lark, pastor of Bethel Mennonite Church, services were started in the Dearborn Street community, thirteen blocks from Bethel. The first service was held in the Isaac home on December 2, 1945, with eight persons present.

Attendance soon began to grow and activities to multiply after the Dearborn Street Mission emerged as a mission outpost of Bethel. On April 14, 1946, the first members were received. The following year a building was purchased and remodeled into a chapel. Dedication was held February 2, 1947.

In 1950 membership had grown to 24 and attendance reached into the 50s. But when Brother Lark moved to the Rehoboth community in the mid-fifties, the church was closed, largely because of the lack of leadership and, possibly, the lack of adequate vision.

Camp Rehoboth (1949) later called Rehoboth Mennonite Church. In the summers of 1947 and 1948, children from the Bethel congregation in Chicago had been sent to Camp Ebenezer at Millersburg, Ohio. Pastor James Lark had a vision for a summer camp ministry and was instrumental in opening this first venture of its kind in the Mennonite Church. Fifteen young people, including a father and mother with five children and another mother and her two daughters, were brought into Bethel as members. All but the father had spent some time in camp.

Because of the distance, the Illinois Mission Board felt that they should not continue to send children to Camp Ebenezer. Brother and Sister Lark believed, however, that some sort of program should again be carried on. But the problem was where they could send the children if not to Ohio. They prayed much about this burden. With faith, they knew that God would open the way.

While the summer activities were getting underway in 1949, Brother Lark received word from a Mrs. Daily that she had ten acres of land near Hopkins Park, sixty miles south of Chicago, that she would sell for a campsite. This seemed an answer to prayer. Brother Lark found the plot suitable and bought it. The land was a wooded area quite appropriate for camping, but the question of buildings remained to be solved. In response to a call from Brother Lark, a carload of men from Goshen, Indiana, came and put up a frame building. This served as a kitchen and dining room. In less than two weeks from the time Brother Lark obtained the land, the necessary equipment had been provided to begin camp.

Several of the Bible school teachers who had been teaching at the Bethel church in Chicago volunteered to staff the camp. In a short time children from Chicago were enjoying the free open air where they had lots of room to play. Interspersed in the activities were daily periods of Bible study and work chores.

The community at Hopkins Park was made up of mostly rural black people. A survey of the area revealed the need for a Christian ministry. It seemed the Lord had opened the way to have that camp located in such a community.

In November 1949, Brother Lark and several workers led the first service with 13 present. Additional meetings were held in the camp house with sufficient interest to continue the work.

In Chicago, on December 21, 1949, a disastrous fire swept the lower part of the dwelling in which the Larks and other workers lived. No other suitable living place could be found in the city so the household moved to the camp. Brother Lark had already been working to get the camp house in sufficient shape to live there permanently. The house was raised and an addition built. It again seemed that the Lord was providing.

Since the Larks and the workers lived at the camp they were able to do more effective work in the community. They started a weekly adult Bible class for which Sister Lark served as teacher. They also undertook a visitation program. Meanwhile, the Larks continued their primary responsibilities at the two churches in Chicago.

In October 1955, a new building for a nursery and kindergarten was built on the campground. Later, ground was broken for a new church. At this point, Mark and Pauline Lehman came to assist. Mark was ordained as pastor in 1956, and in 1962 the congregation completed an addition to the sanctuary. In 1986 the membership was 58.

Michigan

Ninth Street Mennonite Church (1949) Saginaw is largely an industrial city with several General Motors plants and foundries. Le Roy Bechler's vision for a summer ministry there resulted in the invitation from persons in the black community to conduct a summer Bible school.

In the summer of 1949 he led a Voluntary Service unit in conducting a Bible school that attracted over 200 children. The children were invited through personal contacts and visitation in homes. Through the Bible school efforts, 28 persons made a profession of faith. Though the original goal was not that of planting a church, it became evident that the door was open to do so.

To facilitate the founding of a permanent witness, a local board was formed of interested members from several nearby Mennonite churches. This group purchased and remodeled a house for worship services, and on November 20, 1949, the first Sunday service of the Saginaw Gospel Mission—later Ninth Street Mennonite Church—was held. In August 1950, Le Roy Bechler and Irene Springer were married. In December of the same year Le Roy was ordained to the Christian ministry.

The following year a lot was purchased and a church was built and dedicated. The major focus of the ministry was on the youth. The first baptisms for membership included a mother and her children. Efforts with the youth and children eventually attracted a number of adults into membership.

Summer Bible school outreach into nearby communities led to the planting of another church by Melvin and Lois Leidig. In 1955 Melvin Leidig was ordained as pastor. This church is now known as Grace Chapel.

Following the first two pastors, Lee Arthur Lowery from the congregation was ordained and served as pastor at Ninth Street from 1972-81, after which he resigned for further training. Currently deacon Grover Hollis, Sr., serves as congregational leader.

In the fifties the congregation purchased a house several doors from the church as well as a vacant lot behind the church facilities. Under the leadership of Pastor Lowery, an addition was added to the church building and parking lot. In 1986 the membership was 43.

Ohio

Mennonite Gospel Chapel (1947) renamed Rockview Mennonite Church. Youngstown was at one time considered one of the largest steel centers in the nation. These mills attracted large numbers of people from the South.

Members of the Leetonia Mennonite Church near Youngstown became interested in the spiritual needs there. They began to visit the community on Sunday afternoons, telling Bible stories on the porches, in yards, or wherever a group gathered. The congregation rented a building and held the first service on November 2, 1947. As the ministry developed, the Leetonia congregation took sponsorship and supplied workers.

In 1949 the Leetonia congregation provided a more adequate rental building. There was no pastoral leadership, however, and no members were received until the early fifties. In 1954 Fred and

Carolyn Augsburger responded to the call to serve as leaders at the Gospel Chapel. Augsburger led the congregation in the purchase of a lot and church building which took the name Rockview Mennonite Church.

In 1962 the Augsburgers were instrumental in planting a second church, Berean Mennonite, where they served until 1981. Wilson Baatuma is the current pastor there. Following another pastor at Rockview, Charles McDowell became the congregation's first black pastor in 1965. In 1986 membership at Rockview was 33 and at Berean 26.

Gladstone Mennonite (1948) later Lee Heights Community Church. Cleveland, with all the characteristics of the large city, offered a fertile field for evangelism. Tillie Yoder, an energetic Christian, believed that the Mennonite Church had something to offer the black population.

In the winter of 1948 she made several investigative visits to Cleveland to explore the possibilities of ministering in the black community. She received a positive response in two suggested areas, each with a public school available for use as a facility for holding summer Bible school.

She immediately asked for churchwide Voluntary Service's help and received assurance that a unit would be provided to spearhead a ministry in this new field. On June 21, a volunteer unit of six persons was organized. The members of the Plainview Mennonite Church, 20 miles south of Cleveland, offered a place for them to live and furnished food and transportation into the city.

The VS unit first concentrated on the Gladstone community where over 330 pupils enrolled for the first Bible school. From there the unit held a Bible school in the Mayflower community. Enrollment was 349, and 22 young people made professions of faith. Impressed by this kind of interest, the Plainview congregation appointed a committee to give guidance to a follow-up effort. Member Allen Stutzman, along with several others, went into the Gladstone community for Sunday afternoon Sunday school.

Following another summer of successful summer Bible schools, a group of children was taken for a two week camp-out at Camp Ebenezer in Holmes County, Ohio.

In 1954 Vern and Helen Miller accepted leadership responsibilities and Vern was installed as pastor.

He led in setting up a ready-made steel building where services were held until land was secured and new facilities were built in the Lee Heights community. This middle class community was ready for the witness of Lee Heights Church, and the membership soon began to grow. By the late seventies the congregation had established a day-care center and built a sizable addition.

Lee Heights has taken on a community church approach, with many members not holding membership in the Mennonite Church. Individual members are, however, free to affiliate with the church. In 1986 the membership was 329.

In 1963 Warner Jackson, a member of the congregation, was ordained to the ministry. He also established the University Euclid Fellowship in 1970. In 1986 membership there was 40.

Ten observations at this juncture° can be made which, together, suggest something of the spirit and substance of black Mennonite outreach before 1950:

Highlights, 1898-1950

1. The first known black members, Robert and Mary Carter, and their son, Cloyd, were received into the Lauver Mennonite Church, Cocolamus, Pennsylvania, in April 1897. They were reached through evangelistic meetings.

2. Lancaster Conference, through the lay-led Lancaster Sunday School Mission (established 1894), was first to reach the black communities with a witness.

3. The first intentional involvement of the Mennonite Church with blacks was in 1898 when the Welsh Mountain Industrial Mission was established.

° *Note:* A fuller treatment of the present scene for Mennonite blacks, including current congregational goals, would be helpful. Such a survey should be prepared by a black writer. This larger perspective is needed for each of the congregations in this chapter. The purpose of this chapter has been to emphasize mission beginnings before 1950.

4. The next mission was established in 1933 in Lancaster, Pennsylvania, 35 years later. The work did not begin with the intention of planting a church in the black community. When blacks began attending the all-white churches, a separate church was started, known as the Lancaster Mission for the Colored.

5. The first intentional effort to plant a witness in a black community came in 1935. The Young People's Christian Association at Eastern Mennonite College established the Broad Street Mennonite Church in Harrisonburg, Virginia, as a Christian service project.

6. A total of 13 missions were begun between 1898 and 1950 that ministered primarily in black communities. Five of these were established in Lancaster Conference in Pennsylvania. Eight were begun in the nineteen-forties, seven of these outside of the Lancaster Conference.

7. James H. Lark from Quakertown, Pennsylvania (Rocky Ridge Congregation), was ordained in 1945 at the Bethel Mennonite Church, Chicago, Illinois, as the first black Mennonite minister and in 1954 as the first black bishop.

8. Lark was the first pastor at Bethel Mennonite Church, Chicago, and established two mission outposts at Dearborn Street in Chicago and Rehoboth at St. Anne, Illinois. Rehoboth began as a summer camp.

9. Of all the 13 missions prior to 1950, black membership was largest in the Bethel and Dearborn Street missions, both led by Pastor Lark.

10. The emphasis during these years focused more on *doing* mission work—the practical aspects of social and spiritual ministry—than in planting churches in which black and white became true brothers and sisters in fellowship with each other and the larger church.

6
WEIGHING THE EVIDENCE

Although recent black Mennonite history, since 1950, may be chronicled, it is still too early to attempt to interpret it in all its depth. From the standpoint of 1986, two things, however, still need to be attempted—in themselves, a sort of interpretation of black Mennonite mission up to 1950. These are: (1) compiling statistics up to the 1980s, and asking certain questions of the charts and facts; and (2) describing three model congregations that seemingly have found a degree of success in the goal of establishing groups that are both indigenous and self-supporting.

The statistics, charted in various ways in the Appendix, are analyzed in this chapter. The three models are the focus of chapter seven. Throughout these last two chapters I have also, consciously, attempted to communicate my own views and vision, sometimes posed more in the form of a question than in attempted, definitive answers.

Statistics

The following tabulations summarize the charts in the Appendix. What does the evidence tell us from a church growth perspective?

1. The average annual growth rate of black membership since 1950 is 8.2 percent. However, of the 42 Black/Integrated (B/I) churches established before 1970 the average annual growth rate from 1970 to 1980 was 1.41 percent, a decline of 6.8 percent. The decadal growth rate was 15 percent.

Here is a rule of thumb table on evaluating church growth:

25% per decade (2.256% AAGR°)—Biological growth only: poor
50% per decade (4.137% AAGR)—Fair for U.S. and Canada
100% per decade (7.177% AAGR)—Good for U.S. and Canada
200% per decade (11.612% AAGR)—Excellent for U.S. and Canada
300% per decade (14.896% AAGR)—Outstanding for U.S. and Canada
500% per decade (19.623% AAGR)—Incredible for U.S. and Canada

2. Fifty-three percent of the B/I churches were established in the 1940s and 1950s, 22 percent in the 60s, 12 percent in the 70s and 2 percent in 1980-82. In fact, more B/I churches were established in the 40s than in the 70s and early 80s combined. What factors have contributed to this decline?

3. Thirteen B/I churches, or 31 percent, had a membership decline in 1980.

4. Only one church has a membership over 100.

5. The Lee Heights Community Church has adopted an interdenominational approach and has become the largest of the B/I churches in the Mennonite Church. It has had a phenomenal growth since its beginning in 1947. Its decadal growth rate in 1970-80 was 38 percent, while the decadal growth rate of the B/I churches was 15 percent.

6. The patterns of growth, though growth in the B/I churches may have exceeded that of the whole denomination, are, nevertheless, reflective of that of the denomination.

7. 1,624 black members make up 1.6 percent of the U.S. Mennonite Church membership of 1.5 percent of U.S. and Canadian membership. There are a total of 49 B/I churches, and 14 white churches with 4 percent of the black membership.

8. Thirteen conferences, or 37 percent, have black members from black or integrated churches. Sixty-seven percent of our conferences do not.

_____
°AAGR: Average Annual Growth Rate

9. Lancaster Conference has 16, or 33 percent, of the B/I churches with 323, or 20 percent, of black membership. Ohio Conference has 5 to 10 percent of the B/I churches with a membership of 399, or 25 percent, of the black membership.

10. Five B/I churches are located west of the Mississippi, while ten are in Southeastern states. There are none in eight of the Southern states.

11. In 1980 there were 36, or 73 percent, more B/I churches than in 1950.

12. In 1980 there were 1,474, or 91 percent, more black members of the Mennonite Church than in 1950.

13. Nineteen B/I churches planted before the 1960s have less than 50 members. This is 39 percent of the B/I churches.

14. In 1950 there was one black pastor; in 1982 there were 26. None, however, are serving all-white churches.

15. The average B/I membership per church is 32; in the Mennonite Church as a whole it is 88.

Church growth potential

The black population in the United States is estimated to be approximately 26 million. It is said that from a third to one-half of that number is unchurched. There is obviously great potential for the Mennonite Church to reach out and grow.

As members of the Mennonite Church and the body of Christ, we take seriously the Great Commission of our Lord to "go into all the world and make disciples" (Mt. 28:18-20). This has meant going to all peoples, regardless of culture or language.

Witness in the black community began in 1897 by the Mennonite Church. How successful in church planting and discipling has the church been? Has the church been able to bridge the homogeneous unit by incorporating blacks into its life and ministry?

From the believers church perspective, has the Anabaptist

theological position affected the Mennonite Churches' cross-cultural outreach? Its incorporation of blacks into the life and ministry of the church? Its racial attitudes?

The melting pot ideal for American society has been largely called a myth. Is the melting pot also a myth as far as Mennonites are concerned? Can the church successfully bridge cultures? What is our track record?

Why are some churches healthy and growing, while others are stagnant and dying?

Why are some churches hard pressed to find space for people, while others struggle to keep the machinery going?

How can Mennonites effectively minister to black Americans? What factors must be present? What changes must be made?

We have a great deal to learn from the black church in general when it comes to establishing and planting black Mennonite churches in the inner cities and the urban sprawls. These churches are indigenous in their context and are not reliant on either mission boards or subsidies to keep alive. Subsidies and mission boards seem characteristic of the white denominations trying to bridge cultures. This is not to minimize the hundreds of thousands of dollars and untold numbers of hours given to share Christ's love in witness and service. We must remember, however, that while we as a church are struggling to reach out to black communities, black churches themselves are abundantly growing.

Defining the black church

I believe we can learn much from the black church and her role that will help us to be a part of the church reaching the black community for Christ.

The general black church evolved, not as a formal black "denomination," with a structured doctrine, but as an attitude, a movement. It represents the desires of blacks to be self-conscious about the meaning of their blackness, to search for spiritual fulfillment in terms of their understanding of themselves, and their experiences as a people in history.

Black religion cuts across denominational, cult, and sect lines to do for black people what other religions have not done because it assumes their humanity; it is relevant to their situation; it gives them responsibilities; it allows their participation; and it confirms their right to see themselves as created in the image of God.

What is the ingredient that makes the black church unique? The Christianity projected by the black church is a *humanizing* one, taking into account the social, economic, and political aspects of the world. All of life is incorporated in the worship of the black church as it celebrates the power to survive. The black church has not separated the prophetic function of the church from the priestly one.

Reflections on the Mennonite Church experience

It appears that we in Mennonite Church home missions have had a misconception, or an ill-conceived philosophy of ministry that appears to show through in the statistical results of this study.

We have taken seriously the fact that we are *to do* mission work. The idea has been that the work of ministry is primarily in the *doing* rather than in the *being*. Everything has depended on our doing it. Examples of this include hauling children to Sunday school; door-to-door canvassing; doing visitation work; sharing food stuffs; distributing literature; fixing, building, and maintaining worship facilities; teaching classes; loaning or giving money, and so on. Unless we do it, and do it our way, it won't get done right.

This type of ministry has characterized our attempts at reaching into the black community. A multitude of mission workers and families have faithfully driven into the mission community and have made great personal sacrifices of time and money to help those in need. Now if our philosophy of missions is merely service, then we have been on target. However, if our concern goes beyond individuals' immediate needs, if it desires to help them become the people of God—our brothers and sisters—we must assume a broader role.

Our responsibility is to bring God's inspiration to bear upon those within the context of our lives, to encourage them to discover their identity by finding direction and purpose for their lives. Taking this responsibility will allow us to affirm and equip new saints for the work of ministry.

Our mission boards and congregations have given millions of hours and dollars in *doing* ministry. Why hasn't the church produced more black churches, members, leaders, and pastors?

For example, one of our home missions in one of our nation's largest cities has received since 1950 a total of a quarter of a million dollars in subsidy and hundreds of workers. Today, however, the congregation does not own the building, still receives subsidy, and has an active membership of less than 50. Could it be that this example reveals the type of philosophy we have as a believers church—the belief that it's our responsibility, that we are to *do* mission work?

In the process of serving we have been so intent on the *doing* of ministry that we have failed to inspire and equip the people, so they might also become the pioneers and the workers, thus multiplying the ministry of Jesus Christ. I believe this lesson was learned the hard way by many foreign mission boards who had to revamp their entire method of approach. We need to learn this lesson when crossing cultures as well as when staying within a homogeneous context.

Point by point

Developing relevant ministries in black and integrated communities means that:

1. The socioeconomic factors must be understood when efforts are made at church planting/developing. These factors include underemployment or no employment, family breakdown, lack of quality education, housing needs, and the effects of inflation.

2. The philosophy of ministry is defined. Is it to do mission work or to plant and develop churches? It is important also to have a correct theological concept of evangelism.

3. It is the mission of the church to grow. This means that the church must have a relevant biblical theology, meaningful traditions, adequate facilities, and relevant programs of Christian education and stewardship.

4. A strong indigenous leadership training program, both on a congregational and a denominational level, must be developed and maintained.

5. Black and integrated churches must be allowed to develop ownership. Too close ties with a strong homogeneous group such

as Mennonites can stifle, slow, or hinder church growth and evangelism. In fact, the majority of B/I churches are subsidized; 41 percent of these churches do not own their church facilities; and at least 30 percent do not have a church constitution.

6. B/I churches must become indigeneous within their own cultural context. Patterns of worship and music, for example, should be suited to the culture.

7. We must help B/I churches find ways of identifying with their communities. We must look for the needs.

8. We need to develop and secure the type of leadership that will enhance the effectiveness of the church's mission and ministry in B/I communities.

9. A well-defined strategy for evangelism/church planting in black communities should be developed in the light of growth potential. Up to this point no such strategy exists.

10. Our denominational agencies must give guidance on how to effectively develop cross-cultural ministries.

11. A high priority should be given to the numbers of B/I churches established prior to 1965 that have shown little or no growth. A congregational self-evaluation as a means of developing goals or of determining future ministry is of utmost importance.

We, as a church, have crossed many cultural bridges. We have shared the message of the gospel with diverse peoples, and we have planted churches in unfamiliar soils. But our journey is far from over. New roads beckon us forward with the hope of gaining new companions—an ever-growing fellowship of people in mission.

7

BLACK MENNONITE CHURCH MODELS IN THE 1980s

The Mennonite Church began reaching across ethnic and cultural lines at the beginning of the century. Fifty years later, there were approximately 150 black Mennonites. During the next 30 years, the membership grew to a little over 1,600 members in 49 black and integrated churches. Of these 49, only three were indigenous and self-supporting.

What were the factors in the development of these three churches which aided them in becoming independent? What can be learned from their experiences?

Each of these churches had a different kind of beginning. Calvary of Los Angeles experienced racial transition. As the neighborhood changed from white to black, the congregation struggled for survival, some members withdrew, and a new strategy emerged.

Lee Heights began with Voluntary Service workers living in the Gladstone area and conducting Bible schools in the inner city of Cleveland. Good response led to the establishment of a Sunday school and other service ministries. In the relocation process, an indigenous and interdenominational community approach was adopted.

The third model, Calvary, Newport News, Virginia, began as a mission outpost of the Warwick Mennonite Church, Newport News, Virginia. Drive-in workers heavily supported the church until it was able to assume its own responsibilities some twenty years later.

All three of these churches began with white leadership. The two Calvary congregations have moved from white to black leadership. I believe we can learn much from these three pioneer efforts to plant churches in other ethnic and racial communities.

Calvary Mennonite Church
(Inglewood, California)

In 1912, Mennonites from the Midwest and the East migrated into the Los Angeles Basin. During World War I, they made efforts to start a church, but it was not until 1920, when a Mennonite minister moved into the area from Oregon, that they organized the first Mennonite church in South Los Angeles—Calvary Mennonite. Shortly thereafter, they purchased a lot and built a place of worship.

These Mennonite people were a tight homogenous group, both ethnically and religiously. Calvary was a member of the Pacific Coast Mennonite Conference, a conference which enforced strict religious discipline. Though this discipline caused a certain amount of separation from "the world," the congregation was, nonetheless, deeply committed to the cause of Christ. It ministered to the sick and the needy, organized youth activities, and picked up children for Sunday school.

In the late forties, blacks began to move into the Calvary community. At first little notice was taken, but as the trend continued following World War II, the pastor endeavored to lead the congregation into an interracial ministry. This seemed natural for a church from an Anabaptist theological tradition that stressed love and peace. To transcend the sociological implications of such a ministry, however, was difficult for a number of members and not practical for some who lived outside the church community.

Black children became involved in Sunday school while adults visited but did not become a part of the church. Even when the community was white, few non-Mennonites had been incorporated into the membership. The church became largely a meeting place for Mennonite people living in a wide radius around the church, rather than a community-centered congregation.

In the late fifties, the pastor resigned and a number of interim pastors ministered to the congregation for some time. The congregation considered selling the property and relocating, but through the influence of a black interim pastor, James H. Lark, and with the counsel of the home missions secretary of the Mennonite Church and district conference leaders, the congregation agreed to retain the facilities for a continuation of witness. At that time, a majority of the members decided to leave Calvary. They withdrew in the fall of 1960 to establish the Faith Mennonite Church in Downey, California.

In January 1961, Le Roy and Irene Bechler and family moved into the parsonage to assume leadership of Calvary. Since the growth of the congregation until then had been largely biological or due to Mennonite transfers, the first step taken by the new pastor was to lead the church to draw members from the community. He encouraged members to become identified with community needs and concerns. At that time, the local schools were fast becoming all black, a change which meant that many local community organizations like the Parent Teacher Association would need to be rebuilt. The involvement of the pastor and the church in this organization brought a positive response from the community and, as a result, increased attendance and membership. Growth and its opportunity for an enlarged ministry made it necessary to rethink facility needs. At the current location there was no space for off-street parking or building expansion.

In 1969, a beautiful church building, including facilities for a Christian day school, was offered to the congregation and subsequently purchased. This building was sold by a white evangelical church that was afflicted with "ethnikitis" and chose to disband.

For Calvary, a time of readjustment followed the new move. It had been accustomed to operating on a shoestring budget and in small facilities. Since facilities were now adequate to offer a broader ministry to the community, it became necessary to readjust attitudes toward growth.

After regular worship services and related programs were established, plans were made to establish a Christian day school. The poor conditions of the inner-city schools were apparent, but a time of testing came at the opening of the school from several black militants. Their children, because of their color, had been refused admission to the school by the previous denomination. There was picketing and various confrontations occurred. These passed, however, and today over 200 students are enrolled in kindergarten through grade six.

The congregation now has predominately black membership, a condition that reflects the composition of the community.

Calvary's philosophy of ministry (described in its constitution) is:

> To promote religion, charity and education in accordance with the principles and teachings of the Mennonite Church.... To relieve the poor, heal the sick, and aid the distressed and the helpless, and to administer spiritual and physical solace, relief and help to those in need.

Neither the constitution or bylaws specify the philosophy of ministry very clearly. Until the sixties, the congregation was part of a close-knit German ethnic religious group. It emphasized loyalty to the denomination and helping persons in need, but there was little influx from the community.

The church, at that time, served as a regional rather than a community church. Members living as far away as 25 to 30 miles commuted each Sunday. The main outreach ministry focused upon children's activities. Up to 75 children were involved in Bible classes, crafts, and camping. Although this was a service to the community, few of these young people were incorporated into the membership.

After a majority of the congregation decided to relocate, the pastor helped the Calvary church evaluate its basic philosophy of ministry. It decided that as part of Christ's church, its mandate was clear: the church was not there to serve only a part of the community but to minister to the total community, irrespective of race. The congregation recognized that the integrity of the gospel and the church was at stake. Already, integration was a hot issue and this so-called "white church" had been accused of bigotry.

The first hurdle for the church was to identify with the local community—an endeavor that meant a change of attitudes and personal involvement with community people. As a representative of the Savior, the congregation desired to be a caring community of believers. As idealistic as this may sound, the church felt that this was what the gospel is all about.

Until the large exodus in 1960, Calvary's membership was basically one homogeneous unit and could be described as kind, peaceful, loving, thrifty, and mindful of its own business with little or no involvement in the sociopolitical structure around it. The change in the church's philosophy of ministry, however, soon brought blacks into the membership.

Since the church was small and struggling to survive, there was a great need for workers, teachers, officers, and so on. If the church was to grow and become self-sustaining, new members would need to be trained to assume leadership responsibilities. Thus, as blacks assimilated into the fellowship, they felt as if their gifts were welcomed and needed. Although bridging cultural differences has sometimes been a painful experience for the church, both white and black members testify that their cross-cultural relationships have been enriching.

Church organization is vastly different in various denominations of the same ethnic groups, so it should be evident that this is especially true between churches of different racial compositions. In the black church at large, especially among Baptists, the board of deacons is vested with the primary responsibility of administering the church. The pastor, however, is seen as the unquestioned leader, administrator, and executive officer. Also notable are the large number of inner committees, all of which are subject to the pastor and the board of deacons. Calvary, coming from a different cultural background, was not familiar with the religious orientation of those it was trying to reach. Since the pastor was to some degree familiar with it, he endeavored to lead the congregation to incorporate elements of both black church organization and worship into the church.

Before the congregation's racial change in 1960, Calvary Mennonite was considered by the denomination as a financially stable church. After the exodus of a majority of its membership, it had to face the question as to whether a church in a transition community could survive financially. Fortunately, with the assured support of the denomination's missions agency, the congregation received sufficient subsidy to support a full-time pastor. Had this not been the case, the situation would have been much more difficult. The church may have had to sell to a black congregation, take the money, and begin a church of the same homogeneous group elsewhere.

At Calvary, financial giving was not stressed because that had never been the custom there. It took seventeen years for the church to become financially independent. During those years, available finances that came from within and without were used in primarily three ways:

1. To sell the original church facilities and parsonage and to purchase a $150,000 facility that seats over 300 and includes a Christian day school for 230 students, a playground, and parking lot.
2. To purchase a now debt-free five-unit court for senior citizens.
3. To purchase a corner business property and a duplex, both adjacent to church facilities. These are now financially self-supportive.

The congregational giving is now primarily used for the basic operation of Calvary's local ministry and some mission giving.

The church in a changing community needs a special kind of leadership, one which has a missionary vision and is able to cut across different homogeneous units. In a sermon in early 1982 Pastor Hubert L. Brown said, "The only reason we exist is for the salvation of souls. We are called to transform our communities from crime to Christ, from despair to hope." To those hesitant or unsure about how to introduce Christ to others, Brown said, "The Bible says if you only call on the name of Jesus you can be saved. We are talking about eternity in the balance." For the first six weeks of 1982 congregational members were encouraged to undertake an each-one-reach-one effort. The church's Community Outreach Commission led in this effort.

Other ministries of the congregation are coordinated by four commissions: Christian Education, Church Management, Gathered Life, and Pastoral Ministries. The latter two commissions are new since Pastor Brown came in 1980 and deal with enriching the church's life as a worshiping community and with helping the pastor minister to members in crisis. Caring groups of six members each function under the guidance of Pastoral Ministries.

Members have clearly responded positively to the teaching of the Word. When it became evident in the early sixties that Calvary would only survive if the blacks assumed positions of responsibility, God led to Calvary many persons whose gifts strengthened the church's ministry.

At Calvary, members make a conscious effort to be flexible, to be open to new cross-cultural ways of worship and ministering. In each Sunday morning worship service, Mexican Americans, blacks, and whites worship together. Sometimes the Chicanos will sing in Spanish with the congregation occasionally joining them in a chorus. Or special music may include white and black choir members singing soul music. Calvary has chosen to be pluralistic—open to all kinds of persons with varying lifestyles. The primary concern is not to build a Mennonite way of life or impose a certain piety upon those who are reached; it is to seek ways of being God's people today, involved in his mission in his world.

Furthermore, the composition of the congregation is unique. Of the 80 members who are considered relatively active, approximately a

Calvary Mennonite Church
Inglewood, California

Myrna Kramer (left) and the first members from the community, Dessie and Sylvester Joyce.

Pastor Le Roy Bechler greeting Calvary worshipers as they leave a service in the 1960s.

Pastor Le Roy Bechler (left) and trustee chairman Charles Jordan at the five-apartment hous-ing unit purchased by Calvary in 1964 for senior citizen occupancy.

The summer Bible school teaching staff at Calvary in 1963.

The Calvary youth choir directed by
Irene Bechler.

The Calvary Mennonite Church facilities purchased in 1969 from a white evangelical congregation which chose to disband.

A chapel period of Calvary Christian School meeting in the auditorium of the church.

Calvary pastor Hubert Brown preaching on a Sunday morning.

Calvary's senior citizens' group on a visit to the Forest Lawn Memorial Park, Los Angeles.

The back side of Calvary Mennonite Church with the new school addition in the foreground.

third are singles. Combined with the number of families where one spouse is a member, half of the active membership is singly involved within the congregation. The congregation is attempting to reevaluate and adjust the church's mission to its various groupings.

One dilemma Calvary has faced is that in many families both parents are employed out of economic necessity or members are furthering their education. This in itself is not bad, but if priorities are not kept in proper perspective, the church is hindered from involving many of its members in ministry. The spirit is willing, but many times the flesh is tired.

A majority of members come from denominations other than Mennonite. This is to be expected, since the Mennonite Church is largely unknown in the black community. An on-the-spot survey indicated that a majority of adult members came into the fellowship by personal invitation. These people say the reason they continue as members is because of the love, warmth, and concern that is shown and because the Word of God is taught clearly and spiritual needs are met. One has to understand that many in the black community, as well as in white churches, have not had much exposure to solid Bible teaching or preaching. Over and over again, members have expressed appreciation that at Calvary Mennonite Church discipleship becomes meaningful and more fully understood.

The Calvary congregation has a strategic location for ministering. A recent community analysis estimated that 37,000 people live within a one-mile radius of the church. Homes around the church sell for upwards of $100,000 and are well maintained. Of the people living near the church, at least 57 percent, or 21,000 persons, have little or no vital church relationship. Within a three-mile radius, that number is estimated to be over 60,000 persons. Inglewood today represents a stable community of mostly blacks, a few whites, and a growing number of Hispanics. With the biblical mandate to evangelize and disciple, the potential is present for real church growth.

The congregation has experimented with several evangelism outreach programs. During the sixties, the most effective outreach tool was the home Bible studies. These were held in the homes of prospective members, many of whom had children enrolled in Sunday school. Home visits gave the church an opportunity to know the community on a personal one-to-one basis.

The other effective tool has been the Lay Evangelism Explosion Training Program. The greatest membership growth occurred the year this program was active. Members going out, sharing their faith, and looking for a positive response were not disappointed. The next two years after the program was discontinued, membership declined. This was partly because steps were taken to consolidate and disciple those who had been reached by the lay program through the use of group Bible studies or cell groups. Success through those means has been achieved by a great many groups, especially in white circles, but not in black churches. This is not to say this strategy cannot be successful in a black community, but it has not been effective at Calvary.

The most long-range, consistent ministry of outreach at Calvary has been its Christian elementary school. The church became interested in ministering to the total person, not to just the spiritual dimension. God seemed to be leading in this effort, one of the most exciting ministries Calvary has ever had. Even picketing by a black militant group failed to hinder the opening of the school. It began with 39 students and for several years doubled in size each succeeding year. Recent enrollment has been over 200, with students in kindergarten through sixth grade. Although the annual operating budget exceeds $250,000, the church has not experienced any financial difficulties. At the same time boys and girls are receiving an education from a Christian perspective, many of the families of those students are touched by the ministry at Calvary.

To look back over Calvary's growth rate since 1961, one sees a steady growth pattern in the sixties, a plateau in the early seventies when the church relocated, and then several years of significant growth followed by a decline. One of the factors which has affected this decline has to do with the church's attitude toward growth. In the fall of 1969, the move to large facilities was traumatic for both pastor and members. The pastor had never been involved in a growing church, and church growth had not been a part of the denomination's emphasis. Calvary suddenly went from small facilities to facilities that had a capacity of several hundred for Sunday school. It was difficult for the congregation and the pastor to change their attitudes toward growth; they now had to think "big."

The age factor has also affected Calvary's growth. Forty-two plus is the average age of church members. The dearth of young families within the church is perhaps a result of America's recent past. The young married adults are the product of the turbulent sixties. During that decade there emerged, and rightly so, the dignity of the black person, the realization that black is beautiful. For a black, coming into a white-oriented black church with white leadership can pose problems, especially ones of identity. In order to be vital, the church must include young leadership.

Another factor affecting Calvary's growth has been "koinonitis," a people turned in to themselves. Over the years a family-like spirit developed making it difficult for new members to break into the circle. Those who were outgoing or very talented tended to break in more easily, but for the average person it was difficult. Members need to have a strong desire to add people to the church.

Last of all, Calvary showed evidence of "St. John's Syndrome." This syndrome comes when Christianity becomes nominal, having the form, but not the power—the profession, but not the enthusiasm for Jesus. It's a second-generation malady, a loss of first love which characterized the church of Ephesus.

Although Calvary's growth rate has declined in recent years, when compared to that of other churches in the Southwest Conference and, more specifically, to the Faith Church that withdrew from Calvary, it is significantly larger. From 1967-77, Faith Church had a decadal growth of 9.5 percent with an average annual growth rate of .91 percent, and the Southwest Conference had a decadal rate of 28.7 percent, with an AAGR of 2.55 percent. In contrast, Calvary's decadal growth was 93.8 percent with an AAGR of 6.8 percent. These figures reflect the fact that church growth in the Mennonite Church for many years was not given serious consideration, and, consequently, growth was not experienced to any large degree. This is not to say the church was antigrowth. The church was not challenged, however, to take a good look at itself in the light of church growth principles.

It is noteworthy that Calvary, a predominately black church in a predominately black community, reflects greater growth than any of the other churches in the Southwest Conference. For these white churches, the growth is primarily biological and by transfer from other churches.

Calvary Mennonite Church has clearly survived the effects of a changing community. Today, however, it still is made up mainly of one homogeneous group, but this time black. In his missionary sermon in early 1982 Pastor Brown recalled his own position on urban mission of not too many years before. "I had quietly given up on the city," he said. The call from the congregation, however, took hold of him. Calvary Mennonite Church, Pastor Brown said, is well located and equipped for an effective reach in winning persons to Christ. It has an expensive and attractive facility. It has a vision. It has a small but able body. It has witness and ministry efforts in place. It has a sense of the wider church. It has experience and history on which to build. Calvary church, he said, has the calling to be a New Testament church, to reach out in Jerusalem and beyond just as "Jesus went about all the cities and villages."

Lee Heights Community Church
(Cleveland, Ohio)

In 1946 the Jake Yoder family from Kokomo, Indiana, bought a farm in Holmes County, Ohio. That same summer their daughter Tillie volunteered to teach Bible school at the Bethel Mission in Chicago where James H. Lark served as pastor. Faced with the challenge of meeting the needs of black urban children, Tillie developed the dream of a summer camp on her father's farm. She shared her vision with the Larks who immediately recognized the potential of such a ministry. Later that year, while on Christmas vacation from college, she talked with her father who affirmed the idea of a camp on his farm.

Tillie next told her plan to Laurence Horst, then director of Voluntary Service for Mennonite Board of Missions, Elkhart, Indiana. With his help and the assistance of neighboring churches, Camp Ebenezer was formed on the Yoder farm in the summer of 1947.

Because she lacked finances, Tillie was unable to return to college the fall of 1947. Instead, she took a job at Wooster, Ohio, and at the same time planned ahead for the next summer's camp. When the opportunity arose for her to go with some friends to Cleveland, she had them let her off in the black ghetto. As she walked from place to place, Tillie eventually found a school and was able to talk with the black principal concerning her vision of a Bible school ministry in Cleveland. When the principal told her that the public schools were available for use, she immediately went to the board of education's office and was given an application.

Tillie asked for help from the Plainview Mennonite Church at Aurora, Ohio, about 25 miles south of Cleveland. This congregation was ready to assist her in supporting a Voluntary Service unit that would hold summer Bible school in the Gladstone and Mayflower schools that coming summer of 1948.

In the 1940s the Gladstone and Mayflower communities were described as probably being the world's worst slums. The vast migration from the South during World War II brought about a severe shortage of adequate housing. Discrimination and segregation gave blacks little choice but to move into slums. Many of the houses were owned by absentee landlords who were interested primarily in collecting their rents.

That summer of 1948, over 400 children attended summer Bible school. Tillie describes the Voluntary Service unit of four as being flabbergasted by the response.

Another ministry that summer involved taking black children to Camp Ebenezer. This camp was a pioneer among Mennonite Church camps and the forerunner of Camp Luz, now operated by the Ohio Mennonite Conference.

During its first summer, the Mennonite Voluntary Service unit in Cleveland related closely to the rural Plainview Mennonite Church. Plainview members provided the workers with living quarters and food from their gardens. On the last Sunday in July, the VSers gave an evening program in which they shared their hope that the Plainview Church would become directly involved in the Gladstone ministry. They asked the congregation to consider sending workers into the Gladstone community who would learn to know the heartfelt problems of the people there and to share the love of Christ.

In that service God touched the hearts of Ray and Vada Stutzman. Vada Stutzman recalls that later that night, after the children were tucked into bed, Ray said, "I've been thinking; I aim to do my part in keeping the work going. We could go up to Gladstone on Sunday afternoons for a start. Some of the young people will go along. At least we can get the children together, even on the schoolhouse steps, and sing with them and have stories with flannelgraph."

Vada agreed, and the ministry at Gladstone was able to continue.

The Stutzmans, with their five children, began leaving their 200-acre dairy farm on Sunday afternoons and driving the 25 miles into Gladstone. They first met with the children on the school steps until the weather turned cool in the fall and then the Plainview congregation rented the school so services could be held indoors. Each Sunday one of the ministers from Plainview and usually several assisting church members joined the Stutzmans.

The workers followed up Bible school and Sunday school contacts with home Bible studies, sewing classes for mothers, and young people's activities. It did not take long for the Plainview visitors to win a responsive reception in the community. A number of young teenagers who had become Christians began to grow in their new-found faith.

Each summer a Voluntary Service unit came to assist in conducting summer Bible schools and youth ministries. In 1951 a large house in the community was purchased and renovated into living quarters for the VS unit and into a center for youth activities. This house gave the mission a more permanent status.

Realizing the potential of this newly opened mission in the inner city, Vern Miller, a student at Goshen College who had already assisted in the summer Bible school program, accepted the call to give leadership. After his graduation from Goshen and marriage to Helen Hostetler in the summer of 1952, Vern and Helen made their home on the second floor of the VS house. In time, this house became a sort of community center. Youth came there for recreation and club activities led by VSers or the pastor.

During this period, a number of 1-W fellows (conscientious objectors to the military draft) were serving in various community service projects throughout Cleveland. Among them was Gerald Hughes, a student at Goshen College, whose home was in rural Pennsylvania. At first, the city of Cleveland did not appeal to him. "I would never live in Cleveland. These people are crazy," he said. Before graduation from Goshen College with a major in music, Gerald had become director of the Gladstone youth center and had married one of the VS women. Later, he not only had a vital role in the emerging church in Gladstone, he also served as a minister of music at Lee Heights Community Church.

Gladstone organized its first church council on April 26, 1953.

The membership, which had reached 35, was represented primarily by community persons, and the majority of workers now lived in the community. Drive-in workers had stopped coming shortly after the Millers took over leadership.

Increased attendance of more than 100 by May meant that larger and more permanent facilities were needed. In the summer of 1953, a building committee was appointed to begin planning for a new building. To assist this grassroots movement, the Mennonite Board of Missions purchased a lot in the vicinity—at 5208 Julia Avenue.

The church itself largely undertook the fund raising for the new building. Gerald Hughes and a young men's quartet traveled to a number of churches, giving programs and receiving freewill offerings for the building project. By July, the congregation began to take two building fund offerings per month. Construction began the first week in September of 1953 and was completed by late fall at a cost of $10,000.

From 1948 through the early fifties, the summer Bible schools attracted hundreds of young people. As the Gladstone congregation grew, the Voluntary Service unit was gradually phased out. The local church now carried on the various ministries, including summer Bible school. Older youth of the congregation began serving as teachers, giving talks, and assuming responsibilities where they were needed. The church became a training ground for future leaders.

During these years, camping played a vital part in the lives of scores of community youth. Tillie Yoder's vision of a spiritual ministry away from the inner city continued to bear fruit in Gladstone's summer program.

In the early fifties, rumors surfaced that the entire Gladstone community would be affected by a comprehensive urban renewal program. Pastor Miller began to prepare the congregation for the eventuality of change and disruption. He also began to make plans to establish another church in a new community to which members could choose to move once they had to leave Gladstone. Mennonite Board of Missions bought a house as a base for the Miller's work in the Lee-Seville area. Gerald Hughes assumed leadership responsibilities at Gladstone until it closed on July 22, 1959. Many members became involved in the development of the new Lee Heights congregation.

The Lee-Seville area of Cleveland, with its rapidly growing interracial middle class, offered the potential for developing an interracial congregation. Mennonite Board of Missions advanced money to buy a house at 4619 E. 175th Street, and in September, 1956, Vern and Helen Miller moved into the community. The planting of an inter-racial interdenominational church, they projected, would bring a certain amount of stability to this transitional community.

The Millers spent the first few months developing a comprehen-sive mailing list of families within a designated area. Two months prior to the first service, they began sending a mimeographed weekly newssheet to every home. Their advance work also included in-person community contacts and regular home visitation.

They rented the centrally located Clara Tagg Brewer School for the first service on the afternoon of December 8, 1956. When only two persons from the community came to the meeting, the workers realized that for the church to take root, a number of hurdles would have to be overcome. Since many of the whites in the community were Catholic and the neighborhood was in transition, a certain amount of skepticism existed on the part of local blacks concerning the intentions of a white minister beginning a new church.

Over the next several Sundays, however, one of the members from Gladstone brought to church some of his relatives who lived in the area. Within several weeks, a nucleus began attending. These people liked what they saw and heard. New people began coming who eventually invited their friends and neighbors to attend, too. Before long, attendance began to reach forty persons a week.

The church directed its main outreach to adults. Early services consisted only of worship, and it was not until much later, when those attending expressed their willingness to assume leadership responsi-bilities, that a Sunday school was started.

The Lee Heights congregation formally organized on September 29, 1957. The 28 charter members first called themselves the Protestant Inter-Racial Parish, but then later changed to Lee Heights Community Church. Lloyd Kenny was elected as the first elder.

That same year, when it became evident that the school would be inadequate, Pastor Miller found two lots in a good corner location on Lee Road. Money to pay for the lots came from the sponsoring Mennonite Board of Missions. Later, two additional adjoining lots were purchased.

The congregation then developed plans to construct a new building. To raise the needed $10,000 the congregation sold bonds at 5 percent interest. These bonds were sold to local church members and friends, as well as to members of the Mennonite Church at large.

Ground breaking was held on August 17, 1958. Under the supervision of Bill Wyse from Archbold, Ohio, volunteers from the congregation and from a number of churches in Ohio faithfully worked at constructing the meetinghouse, a structure which could accommodate 150 persons. The congregation met for its first service in the new building on December 31, 1958, but it did not stop meeting at the Brewer School until February 1959, when the interior work in the new church was finished.

Attendance and membership growth caused the congregation to undertake two more building additions, first an educational wing, dedicated in 1961, and then an enlargement of the auditorium, foyer, and office space in the early seventies. The expansion was funded by member-donated labor, by bond sales, loans, gifts, and funds raised by the members themselves.

Involvement of members in building their own facility opened the way for a stewardship emphasis with the goal to increase budget giving from $12,000 to $20,000 the first year. The involvement ushered in a new era as this congregation, less than two years old in a new location, was well on its way to becoming one of the leading self-supporting "mission" congregations in the Mennonite Church.

As a result of experiences in the Gladstone Church, a basic change in philosophy of ministry emerged in the Lee Heights Church. The new approach was both interdenominational and community based. Shortly after services began, this statement in a bulletin appeared as to "Why a Community Church":

> The community church is an effort to bring all sincere Christians in a given area closer together. It provides an interdenominational worship service dedicated to the proposition that all believers in Christ are brothers. That it is inconsistent for them to be separated in numerous churches.... [B]ecause divided Protestantism is the great religious weakness of our day, this movement is of tremendous importance.
>
> The Lee Heights Community Church teaches all the major doctrines of evangelical Christianity. It is Christ centered and Bible based in its ministry and Sunday school. The church receives subsidy from the Mennonite Board of Missions, but is an independently organized

church without denominational affiliation. It is a self-governing organization with its own constitution and officers.

Staying outside of a denominational framework involved taking financial risk. Fortunately, Mennonite Board of Missions assured the Lee-Seville community church of its support.

There have been several distinct advantages to the interdenominational approach at Lee Heights. It has allowed members a greater degree of freedom and involvement in the political organization of the church; it has given emphasis to the universal character of Christianity, rather than to denominations.

Since the Mennonite Church is largely foreign within the black community, another attractive feature of the interdenominational approach is that it has allowed the church to have a significant ministry without having to work through a selling-the-church process. A Mennonite pastor and several committed Mennonite members have given indirect ties to the denomination.

A major motive of the church planting in the Lee-Seville community was to develop an interracial fellowship. The church was unable, however, to attract local whites, a large number of whom were Roman Catholic. In the ensuing years, the church was also not able to stem the tide of the white exodus nor was it able to attract white Mennonites living in the greater metropolitan Cleveland area. Although it has attracted Mennonite students attending educational institutions, these students have been mostly transient. Interracial couples have also been attracted to the fellowship, appreciating its comfortable atmosphere.

With primarily black membership, the congregation has experienced a greater degree of ownership than otherwise would have been the case. It has been able to become indigenous within its own cultural context, with only certain strands of traditional Mennonite ways showing through the general organization and worship patterns. The overall goal of becoming an interracial church, however, still continues.

Within the black church structure the pastor usually carries a prominent leadership role. Lee Heights, however, determined to give as much leadership as possible to members, and the organizational structure was established so as to let that happen. The pastor is seen as low-key, which allows local community leadership to emerge.

One of the important steps to growth which began at Gladstone was giving responsibilities to youth. Youth from Gladstone have become teachers, worship leaders, and hold other offices. Twenty years later, one of these youth is serving on the trustee board at Lee Heights, and a number of others are serving in various other capacities.

The Lee Heights Doctrinal Statement is consistent with the Mennonite Confession of Faith, but it also clearly underscores the call for the unity of humankind and the belief that activities of racial bigots and segregationists are a clear denial of the Christian faith and love as taught in the Scriptures. The congregation's organization and purpose are designed to meet needs within and without the confines of the church.

At first, it was evident that if the church was to have a significant ministry in the inner city, outside support would be needed. This support came from both the members of the Aurora Mennonite Church and the Mennonite Board of Missions. Subsidy from these two sources allowed the Gladstone church to lay the foundation of the Lee Heights Community Church. In fact, in order for the pastor to give full-time leadership to the church, outside support was given until the mid 1960s when the congregation began assuming full financial responsibilities.

A major milestone in the life of the congregation was reached with the adoption of a stewardship program in 1962. Before the second building program was completed, the church ran out of funds. This brought members to a point in which they had to give serious consideration to the subject of stewardship. Art Meyer, a former student in Cleveland who had become an active church member, shared his vision of what could happen if the congregation took its commitment to stewardship seriously. He introduced the idea of developing a unified budget, a proposal that was well-accepted. For the church newsletter he wrote the following, "Why I Make a Financial Stewardship Commitment":

1. It is in keeping with biblical teaching. Paul said, "On the first day of the week *each* of you is to put aside *something* and store up as he may *prosper*."

2. Jesus said, "Everyone to whom much is given, of him will much be required." Who among us is not eternally grateful for the countless

riches given us? I have been given much (what an understatement!); much is therefore required. This means in terms of *money* also.

3. It is through giving of service and money that I love and am loved.

4. It is through loving others that I am able to love God.

5. It allows the church to better and more systematically conduct her plans of action, nurture, and evangelism.

6. It demonstrates to my children that the church is just as important as the bank to whom I make house payments and the heat, light, and phone companies whose services I pledge to pay for later.

7. It allows me to exercise faith that God will permit me to be able to fulfill the pledge. He has always fulfilled his end of the agreement and to spare.

8. It keeps me giving to the Lord's work when I am discouraged. I wonder about Christians who give only when they're on the "mountaintop," when they *feel* good or must see a tangible need.

9. It is easier to give consistently. I know that the church programs go on whether I am there or not. It costs money to run any institution.

10. Here is one place where I have something to say about how much is given. Last year the federal government income tax took (they didn't ask me) over one hundred dollars more than I pledged voluntarily to the church. I am going to try to give more to God's work this year than Uncle Sam gets via taxes. As you pledge this year, I challenge you to join us in this goal.

Then in 1965, Daniel Kauffman, director of the Mennonite Church Department of Stewardship, was invited to come and introduce a positive stewardship plan to the congregation. This plan included a series of teaching sessions that eventually led to home visitation involving every member. The response was overwhelming; the giving increased from $12,000 to $20,000 in just the first year. This experience points up a valid church principle: when members are given the facts of a situation, they will readily respond. As this happened at Lee Heights, it not only increased the giving toward the budget, but it also brought a greater degree of ownership within the church.

One cannot underestimate the importance of leadership in the

Lee Heights Community Church
Cleveland, Ohio

The Lee Heights Community Church building shortly after completion of the third phase of construction in 1975. The building is bi-level with over 6,000 square feet on each level, mostly for multipurpose use. The auditorium seats 250.

Pastor Vern Miller (left) installing interim pastor Wilma Bailey in June 1983. Rhonda Peery and Ken Sims, president of Community Church and presiding elder at the time, look on.

Gerald Hughes, longtime minister of music, directs the senior choir on the occasion of Community's twenty-fifth anniversary in 1982. Hughes leads congregational singing regularly, assisted by Charles Marshall.

The Lee Heights Gospel Choir. Helen Miller, Laverne Rawls, Michael Winters, and Craig Berkey have served as directors. Pianists have been Rosina Miller Berkey, Gail Banks, and Michael Winters. The two adult choirs sing on alternate Sundays, and the children's choir (Young Voices of Faith) on fifth Sundays.

Eileen Friend teaching Sunday school in the divided Community Room. This room is used by street clubs, political candidates, and wedding receptions as well as daily preschool. Friend, a retired Ohio Bell employee, is also a volunteer helper at the Ministerial Retirement Center.

One of the adult Sunday school classes taught by a team of four teachers: Ray Wentz, Richard Henderson, Herman Moore, and Al Anthony.

The Stewardship Commission at work about 1975. For twenty years this commission has guided Community Church in its giving, facility development, community ministries, and mission benevolences.

Family Night staff in 1978: Chuck and Shirley Jones, Max and Paula Miller, Bessie Wentz, and Lucious Cannon. Wednesday has been family night at the church for many years. The choirs rehearse during the second hour.

Bessie Wentz sharing a Bible story with the junior church young men. Junior church meets twice a month. Wentz is the director of the Hunger Center across the street from the church. It began in the church in 1977 and outgrew its quarters in 1983.

Alice Phillips (left) visiting Queen Boozer, a shut-in. Phillips administers the Golden Rule Day Care Center which occupies three-fourths of the lower level of the church facility five days a week. She has worked there with her staff, cook, and children for over twenty years. Currently she is president of the Missions Society. She has also served the congregation as its Christian education director.

The smiles of four persons who have just visited the Hunger Center indicate how grateful they are for a little assistance. In Cleveland, ten food centers serve hundreds of people weekly, though a client is only eligible six times a year.

In 1983 the congregation was divided into twelve segments for better and closer ministry. Each segment has its own undershepherds. This is a photo of the undershepherds, in charge of coordinator Helen Miller. Feeling the need for better equipped lay leaders, the congregation is helping some persons secure additional training.

The Home Maintenance Ministry is currently carried on by Menno (above) and Melita Penner of Mennonite Voluntary Service. The church has a history of emergency and chronic home repair services given largely on a volunteer basis.

The Children's Choir directed by Sherry Strange in 1978. The choir is still an integral part of the church program. Kim Mack is the current director.

The Ministerial Alliance Retirement Center Board owns and operates this 80-suite building financed by HUD 202 with Section 8 subsidized rent. They are (left to right) Leo Miller, O. Nwaku (United Methodist), Catherine Glenn, George Steward (National Baptist), Vern Miller, and Kenneth Johnson (American Baptist).

Lee Heights Community Church also maintains a counseling ministry, currently carried on by Carol Malone and Vern Miller.

An offender ministry was directed for many years by associate minister John Branham. It is currently in charge of Florence Meeks, a member at Community and director of the work release program at the Cleveland House of Correction.

The church participates in the MCC Summer Student Work program with two local employees. That program is directed nationally by one of Community's former presidents, Pleas Broaddus.

The Philosophy of Ministry at Lee Heights Community Church

"Although we are a ministering rather than a maintaining church body, we do not see service as a substitute for congregational life and mutual ministering. The church seeks to operate a full program of activities for its members and constituents, in addition to its formal community-wide ministries.

"There we may serve from solid care strength as our ministering grows directly out of our congregational life together!

"Evangelism and church growth are an integral part of both our life together and our service ministries. Many join with us because they believe this is the way Christ would have us serve."

growth of Lee Heights. Six years of experience in the inner city had given the Millers a good background for beginning the Lee Heights Community Church. Their foremost goal was to establish an indigenous church, a church that would be self-governing and self-supporting. To do this involved risk, the risk of sharing the decision-making process to allow the church to emerge within its own cultural context.

A general survey of the membership at Lee Heights indicates that members have positive attitudes toward their church. They continue to be part of the church because the preaching and teaching is relevant and because they feel at home there—they have the sense of being loved and accepted. The testimony of one member says it well: "I maybe didn't always agree with the way things were done, but I knew the heart was right."

People want to be part of a church that is reaching out beyond itself, that is trying to meet needs in the community. Lee Heights has provided the avenue whereby such involvements are encouraged. Its ministry is geared to whole persons rather than just the spiritual part. In its original statement of purpose, the congregation declared that one of its goals was to establish a neighborhood church "that meets the practical needs of Christian education and service."

To meet spiritual needs, the congregation has sponsored summer Bible schools, a youth center, and home Bible studies. Unlike the evangelism at Gladstone, however, the main evangelistic focus has been on reaching adults.

At the same time, efforts have been made to deal with some basic community problems, the most critical being overcrowded housing and absentee landlords. The church has also established a day-care center which is operated independently by members of the congregation. Besides providing a wholesome place for children of working parents, the center has given the church visibility.

As the congregation began thinking about where and how the gospel could become relevant in their own neighborhood, other needs have also been met. In an effort to meet hunger needs, Pastor Miller and Rev. Burgess, a local pastor, established the Southeast Ecumenical Ministries in 1978. With the approval of the Ministerial Alliance, contact was made with the Greater Cleveland Interfaith Council, an organization which supports a network of ten hunger centers. The council approved the proposal of a center in the Lee Heights area, and as a result one was set up in the Lee Heights Church. The financial support for this project came from the local Ministerial Alliance and from grants, one of which came from Mennonite Central Committee. The center, which is open three days a week, is directed by a member of Lee Heights who is assisted by a corps of volunteers. It at first served five to six persons a day, but during the recent recession, the number grew to 50-80 persons daily.

Pastor Miller has also been involved in a part-time ministry as a chaplain at what is known as the Workhouse, a job which has given him opportunities to counsel those who have gotten in trouble with the law. His ministry was at one point broadened to include the founding of The Straight-up Half-Way House, located at 1822 E. 89th St., and run under the directorship of John C. Braham. The house provided a place for recently released inmates to begin anew in society. This ministry served its purpose but due to financial problems was discontinued. Rev. Braham, however, continues to serve as a prison worker in the state of Ohio and is now sponsored by the Ohio Conference.

Out of the Ministerial Alliance a family counseling center was also established. The services have since been enlarged to include needs related to alcohol, drugs, vocation, youth, and older people.

To facilitate the concerns of the congregation, a mission committee was formed that has become actively involved in promoting missions. Today, nearly 20 percent of the total church budget is designated for missions and relief. The committee is also involved in visiting shut-ins, convalescent homes, and so on. One of its projects was to send the committee's chairman to Haiti to deliver supplies and to visit the country for eleven days.

Several years after the Gladstone ministry closed and the members became a part of Lee Heights, it was felt that the time was ripe to begin a church in the University-Euclid area of Cleveland. Warner Jackson, a member of Lee Heights and a recent graduate of Goshen College, accepted the call to begin this new church. In 1962 Pastor Jackson, along with a corps of families who were originally members at Gladstone and were now living in the area, organized the University-Euclid Church.

The vision of planting a church in Cleveland Heights also became a reality when Ed Taylor assumed the pastoral role. A meeting place was found and the ministry was carried on for several years. When Ed Taylor accepted a post with Mennonite Board of Missions, John Rogers assumed leadership. Rogers later joined the congregational literature staff at Mennonite Publishing House and this church was discontinued in 1979.

A current goal is to establish a senior retirement facility within the community. Pastor Miller, along with other members of the Ministerial Alliance, has developed plans and filed for funds. Unless there are unforeseen obstacles, this dream should become a reality before the end of the decade.

The Lee Heights congregation is now over 25 years old. There was significant growth the first ten years—16 persons per year—but in the second decade it was 10.2 and the past five years it was 5.6. Why the decline in growth? It should stand to reason that as a church grows in numbers and becomes stronger financially it would maintain a momentum of greater growth. But as often happens, when the congregation reaches a certain peak, a decline sets in.

Although it is true that Lee Heights was planted at a time in which the community was in transition and new people moving into the community were prospective members, I believe there are three major things that happen within a congregation the older it gets that may be contributing to Lee Heights' decline in growth over the past 15 years.

First of all, in many situations, the congregation becomes pastor centered. It is not unusual for the pastor of a black church to be the dominant force within it, whether the pastor is aggressive or low-key. The danger in cross-cultural ministries is that the white leaders in black communities assume a similar role. Generally, their power is even increased since their overall skills are backed with finances and the knowledge of the "right" connections needed in order to get things done. Then, too, the Mennonite Church's teaching on simple lifestyle, love, acceptance, and going the second mile in relationships has considerable appeal. This can unconsciously place a pastor in a very powerful position in the life of the congregation, especially if that pastor is a founding church planter. This may be the case at Lee Heights.

Furthermore, older churches face the danger of institutionalism.

As the pastor at Lee Heights has observed, a large proportion of the congregation are Sunday morning members. Evidence also indicates that only a certain corps of members holds offices within the congregation. Although the organization is there—the programs functioning and the contributions adequate to meet needs—the question still remains: how do you involve and incorporate the membership into an alive fellowship excited to be part of the body of Christ?

Moreover, like many older churches, the Lee Heights Community Church needs to regain a clear vision of its goals. Its first major goal was to plant a church in the Lee-Seville community. It was up to those in the local community to reach out by mailings, door-to-door calls, and follow-up visits. This method worked. The church grew from 28 members in the first year to 168 members ten years later.

The church's next goal was to undertake a building program. This project solidified the emerging fellowship, helping it to assume ownership and serving as a rallying point. Directions were clear and members knew what the end results would be.

In both cases, success depended on how clearly the goals were understood by the group. Because of their clarity, Lee Heights today is a congregation that can serve as a model of what can be done by committed people. But now that the church is planted and facilities are adequate, the question is "what now?" Some are saying the organizational structure of the congregation needs strengthening, the youth program is in disarray, and long-range goals and an emphasis on community outreach are needed. There is a yearning within the congregation to recapture the same enthusiasm that earlier brought a spirit of togetherness.

Lee Heights Community Church is at a crucial point in its history, at a point which requires new vision and strategy for reaching out. It must maintain an inflow of new people and examine anew what it means to be God's people in mission.

Calvary Mennonite Church
(Newport News, Virginia)

In the late 1920s and early '30s, members of the Warwick River Mennonite congregation in Virginia began doing mission work in Newport News. At first they concentrated the efforts in a white community, eventually starting the Huntington Mennonite Church.

Then, in the late 1930s, workers from Warwick began to hold vacation Bible school in as many as four or five black churches every summer. The VBS movement was new and received a warm welcome from the black churches. In 1942, Nelson Burkholder, a dedicated young Christian from Warwick, started serving as Bible school superintendent, a responsibility which he was to have for nearly twelve years.

During the first half of the century, the Virginia Mennonite Conference was reluctant to observe the holy kiss or foot washing of saints with those of other races. In fact, to do so was forbidden by conference action, a decision regretted by some leaders and members who saw this as inconsistent with scriptural teaching on love. Some of these Mennonites had a strong desire to reach out across racial lines and were ready to do so. Their interest was not primarily in black civil rights, nor their aim to protest against segregation and discrimination; their main desire was to share the gospel. When the opportunity to do so was given to members of the Warwick congregation, many black churches graciously opened their arms and hearts to these sincere white Christians who cared enough to offer their programs free of charge.

Nelson Burkholder began venturing into new territory by holding street meetings on Jefferson Street, deep in the black section of Newport News. For weeks he preached the gospel. People who listened wondered, "What are these white folks doing down here?" The message touched some hearts, and there were conversations and follow-up visits. As soon as these follow-ups were made, some blacks began to realize that the white folks from Warwick were, indeed, sincere.

Eventually, members from Warwick decided they wanted to start an interracial church. To begin such a church would be to establish a beachhead in the black community, allowing workers to teach more effectively a new way of love through the cross of Jesus Christ. The Warwick leadership asked Nelson Burkholder to serve such a church. This invitation served to affirm Burkholder's own calling. In 1952 he was ordained to the Christian ministry and began his commission to lead a group of workers in beginning a church in the general area where they had been holding street meetings.

From the positive response at the street meetings, it soon became evident that a permanent place was needed where people could meet and hear the Word. That same year, the Warwick congregation purchased a house which could easily be renovated into a meetingplace.

The first service in the new Madison Avenue Mennonite Chapel was held on November 28, 1952. The workers were ready and waiting, but to their disappointment, only two youth from the community came. This did not dampen the workers' enthusiasm, however, and the service was the beginning of a permanent Mennonite witness.

The following year, a summer Bible school was held at the chapel, and, as the pastor described it, the workers were "swamped with children." Since larger facilities were then needed, a search was begun to find sufficient land on which to build. It was not long until five lots became available on Wickdown Avenue, only several blocks from the chapel. These lots were purchased by funds from friends and members of the Warwick congregation.

A Mennonite building contractor was contacted and plans were drawn up to construct a serviceable building made of cement blocks. One of the young men who worked for the contractor later became the first black pastor of this congregation.

On April 14, 1957, Calvary's first service was held. The church drew primarily teenagers until several years later when a number of adults became involved and eventually joined. Their commitment added stability to the church.

Leslie Francisco, a local black, began attending services in 1958. In 1960 he was made a deacon, and he served in that role until he was ordained to the ministry in 1966. He then assisted Pastor Burkholder as an associate pastor, preaching every other Sunday.

The social crisis of the sixties had its effect on black and white relations at Calvary. There were times of tension between the local community and those driving in from Warwick, and sometimes even points of tension within the church itself. The Burkholders had served the congregation for 22 years, and now appeared the right moment for them to step aside. Leslie Francisco became the new pastor.

This marked a time of transition for Calvary. First, there was the change of pastoral leadership, from a self-supporting pastor to a subsidized one. Second, there was a racial change in the composition of the congregation. White drive-in workers from Warwick ceased coming, and local blacks began assuming leadership roles. Today Cal-

Calvary Mennonite and Calvary Community Churches

Newport News and Hampton, Virginia

The pastoral team about 1972. Front row (left to right): Nelson Burkholder, copastor; Vasco Boyd and Elmer Cobb, deacons. Back row: Leslie Francisco, copastor, and Ernest Godshall, deacon.

The first pastor at Calvary Mennonite, Nelson Burkholder, with his wife, Dorothy.

Calvary Mennonite Church, Newport News, Virginia.

The Calvary Choir singing at Warwick River Church.

Family of deacon Elmer Cobb, at Calvary Mennonite Church, Newport News.

The youth group at Calvary Mennonite Church, 1981.

Deacon Edward James, his wife, Renee (center), and Natalie Francisco. He is also assistant pastor at Calvary Mennonite Church.

Assistant pastor Edward James (front left) and the Calvary Mennonite congregation, Newport News, 1986.

Deacon Steven Francisco, his wife, Karla, and their daughter Tiffany. He is also an assistant pastor.

Veronda Deloacth (singing) and Leslie Francisco at a park meeting in Hampton, Virginia.

A street meeting in Hampton in summer, 1984.

A vacation Bible school group from the Williamsburg Mennonite Church who came to help build the Hampton facility.

God sent help from far and wide to construct the Hampton church building.

The Hampton structure nearing completion in November 1984.

Naomi Francisco and the Calvary Angels Choir singing as they march to the dedication of the new Hampton Community Church.

Stan Maclin (left) and Leslie Francisco cutting the ribbon at the dedication of the Hampton church in May 1985.

Leslie Francisco III speaking at the dedication of the Hampton church.

Left to right: Elder Vernon Doss, Deacon Elmer Cobb, Bishop Leslie Francisco, and Veronda Deloacth (leading music) at the Hampton church.

An evening service at Calvary Community Church, Hampton, in 1986.

Bishop Lloyd Weaver administering the vows to new bishop Leslie Francisco (right). Also present were other bishops from the district, and Joy Lovett (fourth from left).

Leslie Francisco, Jr., pastor of the Newport News church, speaking at Hampton at the installation of his father as bishop.

Joy Lovett (left), associate secretary of the Mennonite Church General Board and staff person for the Afro-American Mennonite Association, greeting new bishop Leslie Francisco and his wife, Naomi.

Bishop Leslie Francisco and Naomi on their twenty-fifth wedding anniversary.

Pastor Leslie Francisco III, with his wife, Natalie.

Personal Reflections on the Work at Hampton, Virginia

Our work here in Hampton came about through a vision that the Lord gave me in 1972-1974. The Lord said, "I want you to build and go forth."

Since then, we have added five classrooms, a nursery, kitchen, pastor's study, two bathrooms, and a second auditorium to the Calvary church in Newport News. The construction work was finished in 1975.

Afterward, the Lord spoke to us about building in Hampton. But first the Lord required us to build up a foundation in Newport News. We began by having street and park meetings in the summer months of 1977, 1978, and 1979 in Newport News. We also held prayer meetings in different homes.

During the winter of 1980, the Lord said, "Now you are ready for Hampton, but Hampton is not ready for you. There are hard-hearted and stiff-necked people—but go." We obeyed the voice of the Lord. We held tent meetings during 1980, 1981, and 1982 and street meetings during 1983 and 1984 in Hampton near my home.

We later purchased two acres from the city of Hampton. We first had to clear the lots before preparing to build. We raised $7,000 in our congregation. Our district also helped with the balance of $20,000. The land was then paid for. We later raised $10,000 in our congregation in order to build. The Virginia Mennonite Mission Board gave us $35,000, the Home Missions division of Mennonite Board of Missions gave us $35,000, and our district gave us $12,000.

John Henry Brenneman and Eli Miller began clearing the lot with a tractor. They are both men from the district and they did not charge a cent for their services. (Praise the Lord.) After the lot was cleared, it was time to dig the foundation and pour the concrete. Brother Buckwalter, who is the pastor of the Upper Room Chapel Mennonite Sea Ministries, helped to lay the blocks for the foundation. Two volunteers came from the Ohio Mennonite Conference came to pour the concrete floor. They poured all but one wing. We poured the remainder ourselves.

Now we were ready to begin the actual framing of the building. Mennonite Disaster Service volunteers from Harrisonburg, Virginia, came to help with the framing of the church. They worked hard but they didn't finish the first week. They returned the second week and finished the job. Two men from Trumbo Electric volunteered to wire the building. My sons put the shingles on the roof. It was actually beginning to look like a church now.

We hired a contractor to come and do the dry walls and the ceiling. Brother Brunk from the Warwick District came and did the plumbing and heating. Sammy Brunk installed our carpet. Bishop Phil Miller from the Chesapeake District built our pulpit and communion table. We bought 150 chairs and did the painting ourselves. Brother Stevie put the windows in and also hung the doors.

On April 27, the last Sunday in the month, we assembled at the place where we had held our street meetings and marched into our new building. Bishop Lloyd Weaver led in prayer on the front steps before we entered the building. Stan Maclin (from one of the Mennonite churches in Peoria, Illinois) and I cut the ribbon, followed by selections rendered by the Calvary Angels and the Calvary Inspirational Choir.

The church was packed with our community people and visitors from the Mennonite churches in the district. Brother Maclin preached a dedication message.

● ● ●

On December 15, 1984, we were called by the Virginia Mennonite Conference to become bishop in the Warwick District. Our job is to serve the two black churches in our district and another black church in the Chesapeake District.

We are now beginning a new work in the Richmond area (fifty miles north of our present church). We will be working with First Mennonite in Richmond. They have agreed to assist us in establishing a black Mennonite church in Richmond.

There are also five black Mennonite churches in North Carolina which we have been asked to visit. They are located in Boone and in Lenoir. Brother R. D. Horton, who is ninety-two years old, is overseer of the five churches in North Carolina. He was my pastor when I was a little boy living there. We don't know at this time if our work will be extended that far, but we are planning to visit them in the future.

• • •

Here at Calvary Community Church we also have a band. It is one of the highlights of our service. The Newport News pastor's wife is in charge of it. Greg Gatling is our drummer. The pastor's wife (Natalie) is our pianist and organist. My son Myron is our bass guitar player. Deacon Cobb's son, Elmer, Jr., is our trumpet player. Darryl Johnson is our saxophone player and Karla (Steven's wife) plays the flute.

We always set aside 15 to 20 minutes at the beginning of our service for praise time. There have been times when the entire service consisted of praise time. I'm saying this to let you know that our band consists of Spirit-filled people and the Lord leads them in their playing.

Our worship service in Hampton is led by an excellent staff. Our usher board has six members. Jessica Morgan is the chairperson. There are ten members in our youth choir led by Steven. We have eight members in our adult choir. My wife (Naomi) is in charge of that. She was once director of the Calvary Inspirational Choir in Newport News.

My son Steven is the assistant pastor here. He also serves on the deacon board with Derrick Gorham. Fran Johnson is the church secretary.

Our church is rapidly growing. For the last month or so, our attendance has been 56 members. We have three more families, along with a sister, who will be joining the church soon. One of these families will be our first white family in the Hampton congregation with a non-Mennonite background.

Yours in Christ,

Leslie Francisco
Calvary Community Church
Hampton, Virginia

February 11, 1986

vary's membership is predominately black and none of the former drive-in workers have felt led to remain an integral part of the church. The hope for an interracial church remains unrealized.

Now that the main financial support was no longer present, the offerings went down. It appeared, as one member recalls, like the church was falling apart. Pastor Francisco, however, would not give up hope. God had given him a prophecy that the church would not fail and the ministry should continue. His bishop asked Pastor Francisco, "Now what are you going to do?" Francisco answered that he was going to be obedient to the Lord.

The church did begin to grow. As it did, additional classroom space, a fellowship hall, and a kitchen were needed. After being discouraged by a lack of outside funds, the church decided to move out on its own. The step of faith brought sufficient funds, and only $13,000 was borrowed. On May 16, 1976, the new addition was dedicated and Simon Gingerich, then secretary of home missions for Mennonite Board of Missions, was the guest speaker. In 1979, the congregation became self-supporting and two years later it assumed responsibility for all pastoral benefits.

Since the change in leadership and racial composition, the congregation has developed a more charismatic approach in its worship services as well as in its church structure. This new emphasis has caused a number of people to leave the church, but at the same time it has drawn others in. No longer does the black community identify Calvary as a "white man's church."

As we look at Calvary, we need to keep in mind that we are dealing with a church that has moved from one cultural orientation to another. As much as we would like to believe that cultural or sociological factors do not have a significant effect upon the church, they do play a vital part in people's response and involvement. We are dealing here with two eras—that of white drive-in leadership and, later, local black community leadership. We need to look at these eras objectively, not with the view that one is necessarily better than the other.

As a witness for Christ and the church as a united body of believers, an interracial church was developed at Calvary. The motives and vision were clear. The gospel that was preached, taught, and lived sought to bring white and black to worship together. The mission witness included children's activities, street meetings, home visitation, and Bible studies. Community people began to sense a love little before felt from white folks. According to one community member, the workers had "so much love for black people, to help the black people.... If there was a need, they would pay for it." This love brought about a certain amount of respect. At first, it attracted the children, and then slowly the adults.

This ministry largely followed the traditional practices of the Warwick congregation. Despite the black community's unfamiliarity with the denomination, the way of worship, church organization, and so on, God used the church to call out a people. A foundation was laid.

Prior to the transition in leadership, it seemed God had been preparing Leslie Francisco for his leadership role. Though he had contact with Mennonites as a child in Boone, North Carolina, Francisco did not become a Christian until the late fifties at Calvary. It was through his sister's children attending Calvary's Sunday school and the subsequent involvement of his wife that he committed his life to Christ. In the late 1960s, he had a spiritual renewal that was to change his ministry. The prophecy came to him that the Lord was calling him to a great work, that some things were going to happen but not to let them hinder him.

This prophecy added a new boldness to his ministry that had formerly been low-key. He led the church from the staid, traditional Mennonite way of worship to a free, lively form. The blacks were responsive to this change, and it brought about a greater identification of the church with the community. Those who had learned to appreciate the traditional Mennonite way, however, soon felt out of place and left.

The role of the pastor also changed. In the black church, the congregation looks upon the pastor as a leader, and it respects him as such. This view of leadership at Calvary has given the congregation a sense of security which has opened the way for it to become self-governing and self-supporting, to be indigenous within its own cultural context.

What is at the heart of Pastor Francisco's philosophy of ministry is "obedience to the Spirit." This philosophy involves taking risks of faith.

Members of the Warwick River Mennonite Church, although

sincere in their obedience to Christ, were never able to transcend their strong Germanic ethnic identity and come to understand the black community. They brought to the city their traditions, beliefs, and interpretations. Because the workers did not live in the community they served, they were often seen as not really interested in the people's basic needs and problems. The relationships between the two homogeneous groups were very much on a surface level.

During that period in history, however, it was difficult for any outsiders to penetrate the inner social structure of the black community. During the height of the black power movement, tension was often felt concerning Calvary's lower church attendance and diminished black involvement. The workers, nevertheless, continued to come, and again and again they endeavored to prove themselves by being kind and helpful.

As mentioned earlier, the dream to begin an interracial church was mostly one-sided. Those who wanted it were Mennonites from the outside. Their goal was both just and biblical, but it is difficult if not impossible to expect to build an interracial church if the community itself does not participate in the vision. The situation might have been different if those who shared this dream had left their suburb, 15 miles away, and moved into the community, thereby becoming an integral part of it.

After the white Mennonites had withdrawn from the church, black members expressed the following feelings:

1. The withdrawal and few return visits indicate that the drive-ins aren't behind us and have little concern.

2. They want us to give programs in their church, but they don't reciprocate.

3. When they thought we needed them, they were here, but when they thought we didn't, they withdrew. This was because they wanted control.

The feelings expressed, however, did not remain the last words on the relationship. The Calvary church has since flourished in an identity and element of its own.

Mennonite churches, on the whole, have a rather simplistic church organization. The pastor is not considered the dominant leader and generally decisions are made by consensus. The structure is clear-cut and the constitution and its bylaws are adhered to. Everything is supposed to be done decently and in order. On the other hand, the black church has been so involved in the total social structure of the community that it has become a unique institution. Sometimes it is difficult to understand its inner dynamics, especially for those from the outside.

On the whole, the pastor of the black church is looked upon as the shepherd and leader. There is a general conception on the part of members that pastors are "called men" of God. They are in the pastoral position because at one point in their lives they received a distinct call, a call so great, they had but one choice—obey. Interestingly, studies made of vibrant, growing black churches indicate there is always a strong pastoral leader. Leadership styles may vary, but there is always a pastor who is confident of his call and who assumes the role necessary to lead the church on to fulfill its mission.

Unlike most white Mennonite churches, Calvary has no church constitution. The pastor, assistant pastor, youth pastor and deacons make up the council, a group appointed by the congregation to make major decisions. Annual business meetings involve the rest of the members in decision making.

A greater degree of ownership was assumed by the members of Calvary when white members from Warwick left and it became apparent that the financial responsibilities were fully theirs. Pastoral leadership challenged the people to tithe and to be obedient to the Spirit. Even children became involved in giving. As the congregation gave, a trust relationship with the Lord developed. There were those who testified that they were on welfare but when they began to obey the Lord in giving they went off welfare. Some were able to purchase a car as well as a home. Tithing was an experience that drew the members together and gave them a new identity—as people of God in mission.

The church made plans in the early seventies to build a much needed addition to their meetinghouse. Although the Lord had given the church a vision to build, leaders in the (district) conference felt the time wasn't right. Calvary's members, however, recognized the Lord's urging and they gave liberally to the addition with both gifts and labor. Grants and a loan enabled the completion of the addition. The

dedication service was, indeed, a time of joyous celebration and satis-
faction for the members.

Steps to become financially independent began to be taken in
the late seventies, and finally in the early eighties the church became
self-supporting. In 1981, the congregation had expenditures of just
under $30,000 and its budget for 1982 was $32,605. Since the average
offering in 1981 was $575, giving had to be increased to a weekly $627
to meet the new budget. The Sunday the writer visited, on October
17, 1982, the offering was $847 and the week before it had been $943.
Though the membership is only about 100, there is a spirit of giving
that dispels the question as to whether or not members can support
Calvary. The wage earners have caught the spirit of giving and have
become deeply involved in supporting the total ministry of the
church.

The leadership style that has emerged in Calvary in Newport
News comes closest to that practiced in the black church. The congregation in the black church tradition sees the pastor as having
received a mandate from God, and thus it shows him a respect that we
in the Mennonite tradition often feel uncomfortable with.

It is characteristic for white leadership in a black community (as
would be the case in any cross-cultural bridging) to do everything
possible to win that community's friendship, to let it know it is sincere.
A leader may do various acts of goodwill, such as fixing a church
window, picking people up for services, or loaning money. One would
not, however, see a black pastor of a black church serving as fix-it man
or errand runner. This, again, is not to say one style of leadership is
better than the other, only that their differences must be understood
and recognized.

At Calvary, the pastor's example and teaching led the congregation to become totally self-supportive. When planning for additional
facilities, it was the pastor who gave the word from the Lord to build.
Members respond to this type of leadership—one which has an ear
open to the Spirit and a readiness to challenge the people to move forward.

The underlying enthusiasm of members gives Calvary strength.
There is first of all commitment to Jesus Christ, and second to the
leadership. On the part of the old-timers there is also great respect
toward the founding pastor and previous workers. According to one

member, "They [the white workers] had so much love for black people and wanted to help them. In essence, they have spoiled us." This same caring expressed by the previous workers characterizes many of the current relationships between members.

Members who feel good about their church are, without doubt, the greatest advertisers for their church. The majority of members first came to Calvary by personal invitation from friends and family. Most of these people were a part of other church fellowships but found some things at Calvary that they hadn't found elsewhere. Reasons members give as to why they continue to support Calvary include: the Word of God is preached and taught; a lot of love and understanding is manifested; physical, mental, and spiritual needs are met; there is a consciousness of God's presence; there is freedom and unity.

For the congregation, the main event of the entire week is the time in which the people of God gather together for worship. Since the change in leadership, the worship service has become much more oriented toward praise. In the beginning, the worship service was very quiet and thus characteristic of the traditional Mennonite service. Community people who were visiting could not understand how people could be so calm, so nonchalant, about worshiping God. People sang out of a hymnbook with no musical accompaniment and the preaching seemed just simply like talk. As the children began coming, they slowly adjusted to this different way of worshiping God, but for older persons it was more difficult.

Pastor Francisco had adapted to the Mennonite way of worship until he had a spiritual renewal. This experience brought a new freedom which transformed his whole ministry. He emphasized the Holy Spirit's role in the life of the church, and he encouraged joyful celebration. Soon, praising God by uplifted hands and clapping became commonplace. One member has remarked, "The Mennonites minimize the Holy Spirit, but it's different for blacks. We have found a new joy and freedom that we didn't have, at least in its fullness."

For blacks, worship has always played a significant role in their lives. Historically, church services have been the only time when they were truly free to be themselves, to exercise their gifts without feeling the restraint often experienced in public. And they worshiped just as long as they wanted to—time was no factor.

At Calvary, the Spirit is present and the congregation desires to see God at work in its midst. By the people's response with "amens," the preacher knows they are with him. It is not unusual to have someone speak in tongues, though when that happens, the congregation waits until there is an interpretation of the message. In the testimony and praise time, at least a half dozen members will stand to share how good God has been to them. At the end of the preacher's message, an invitation is given for those with special needs.

Singing also plays a vital part in the service. It is not uncommon for the congregation to stand and sing praise songs for long periods of time. During the transition experience, with its resulting loss of some musicians, a miracle took place in which persons were given gifts to play. So dynamic were these gifts that during a service it is now common to hear bass guitar, drums, flute, horns, tambourines, and piano.

Calvary has five musical groups, each with its own style, that participate in worship services. In October 1982, the adult choir celebrated its tenth anniversary. This was a festive event that brought together choirs from various churches.

Besides the street meetings, the main outreach for the first 20 years of Calvary's history was the summer Bible school and house-to-house visitation. Bible school gave openings into the homes so that visitation could take place and then, perhaps, eventually a Bible study. In the long run, the most successful method of outreach was the house-to-house contacts.

The desire to evangelize continues to burn within the heart of Calvary's leadership and other members. Members at Calvary feel strongly that God wants the lost to be found and, through its ministries, wants to be part of the search party. Each summer an area in the community is blocked off and the congregation holds a series of street meetings. Besides providing a unique opportunity for lay involvement, these street meetings have led to an outreach ministry in the neighboring city of Hampton where a number of Calvary's members already live. In the summer of 1982, Calvary had a series of outdoor meetings in Hampton assisted by Dorothy Harding, a black gospel singer from Saginaw, Michigan. A number of people at these meetings made professions of faith, and, the following October, ten persons from Hampton were received into the Calvary fellowship. In the hope of planting a church, the congregation purchased two acres of land in Hampton.

In addition to starting a church, Calvary is also exploring the possibility of building a senior citizens complex and a facility to care for delinquents in Hampton. For these visions to become a reality, new leadership will need to be developed and adequate finances provided. The Calvary congregation will also need to replan its strategy in reaching its own church community since the corps of members in Hampton would join the new church and ministries, thus leaving a vacancy at Calvary.

This vision of outreach has caused a certain amount of excitement. The church is mission-minded, venturing out into the world, and its motivation comes from within. (By 1986 the church at Hampton had 29 members.)

From 1952 to 1972, the period during which white workers from the Warwick congregation were assisting the Newport ministry, Calvary grew to a membership of 53. After the transfer of leadership took place, the responsibilities of the church were in the hands of the local community people and membership from 1972 to 1980 grew to 101. In only eight years it nearly doubled. By 1986 the membership was 120.

A number of factors were responsible for the slow growth from 1952 to 1972. One was the local community's feeling of white intrusion. To the members of the Warwick congregation, their motives were sincere in desiring to share the gospel and begin an interracial church, and they did both with a great deal of personal and family sacrifice. To some in the community, however, the situation was seen as outsiders invading their territory. The workers who drove in had basically little in common, either sociologically or economically, with the members of the community; it appears as simply the "haves" giving to the "have nots." Some of the community men and ministers resented this display of charity.

Response to Warwick's ministry first came from the children and youth. They had not yet experienced the full impact of what it meant to be black and did not carry a lot of hurts and frustrations. They were eager to risk, ready to learn, willing to venture into the so-called "white world."

Adult response took longer. Many made promises to come who never came nor even intended to come. There was an air of suspicion, a lack of trust. Some had rejected their own church, so why, they wondered, should they go to a "white man's church"? By persistent teaching and preaching, however, the workers gradually began to break down some barriers. When the breakthrough came, and adults became part of the church, the way was paved for others to follow.

The response was still very small, though, and this was probably due to cultural barriers. The style of worship, the singing, preaching, the role of the ushers, were a few of the areas which were generally done the way the workers were accustomed to. Two particular barriers were the "plain clothes" of the workers which the community found amusing and the absence of musical instruments until more recent years.

The transition from drive-in leadership to community leadership has brought about a greater degree of community ownership and thus growth. As painful as the transition was, it nevertheless opened the way for a church that had been planted as a little mustard seed in the "greenhouse" to be taken out and planted within its own cultural environment.

Summary

We have observed some of the dynamics involved in these three congregations becoming indigenous within their own cultural contexts. Each has provided leaders for the church at large as well as for the Afro-American Mennonite Association. In summary one can observe seven operative principles that have given stability and growth to these churches.

1. The pastors had the gift of cross-cultural ministry. There was much learning by trial and error, but it was the call of God that led them to become church planters.

2. The church identified with the local community. This began earlier in Cleveland than in the other two churches.

3. The churches ministered to the needs within the community.

4. Their aim was to develop a sense of ownership on the part of the people in the community.

5. The congregations wanted to retain the basic Anabaptist theology within the cultural context of the people in the community.

6. The churches have had a strong commitment to evangelism and home Bible studies.

7. Local leadership has been developed.

Many problems commonly faced by a white denomination ministering to another culture have been felt by these churches. Each of them has had to work through these. It is noteworthy that of all the black and integrated churches, Lee Heights Community Church with its interdenominational approach has become the largest, with over 300 members.

The overall challenge posed by the stories of these three congregations is, how can the rich resources of the Mennonites best be harnessed to reach cross-cultural communities? It's a challenge to draw out the best from all our members and from those God would add daily to the church.

APPENDIX

A STATISTICAL ANALYSIS OF BLACK MEMBERSHIP
IN THE MENNONITE CHURCH, 1898-1980

As of January 1980, black and integrated churches had a black membership of 1,624. Mennonite Church membership in the United States was 97,808. There were 49 black/integrated churches and 14 white churches with black members.

The following definitions will help you understand the tables in this appendix:

Black church: black membership exceeds 80 percent.
Integrated church: 20 percent or more black members
White church: 19 percent or less black members

Codes

M	membership	I	integrated
B	black	I/BP	integrated with black pastor
W	white	I/WP	integrated with white pastor
B/P	black pastor	BC	black church
W/P	white pastor	H	Hispanic

District Conferences

A	Allegheny	L	Lancaster
AC	Atlantic Coast	O	Ohio-Eastern
F	Franconia	OQ	Ontario and Quebec
I	Illinois	SC	South Central
IM	Indiana-Michigan	SE	Southeast Convention
IN	Iowa-Nebraska	SW	Southwest
		V	Virginia

Figure 1: Blacks in the Mennonite Church, 1898-1950, 1950-1980

Mission/Church	Conf.	Yr. Est.	Members 1950	Mem. 1970	Mem. 1980	B/Mem. 1980	W/Mem. 1980	Decadal Growth Rate (%)
Welsh Mountain New Holland, Pennsylvania	L	1898	16	36	54	6	48	50
Lancaster Mission—Colored South Christian Street Lancaster, Pennsylvania	L	1933	37	65	50	18	32	-23
Broad Street Harrisonburg, Virginia	V	1935	18	40	48	4	44	20
Diamond Street Philadelphia, Pennsylvania	L	1935	4	42	59	31	28	40
Andrews Bridge Christiana, Pennsylvania	L	1938	47	34	50	2	48	47
Seventh Street Reading, Pennsylvania	L	1938	0	48	65	6	59	35
Thirty-fifth Street Los Angeles, California	SW	1940	5	0				Closed in late 50s
Bethel Chicago, Illinois	I	1944	52	40	56	55	1	40
Dearborn Street Chicago, Illinois	I	1945	24	0				Closed in 50s
Mennonite Gospel Chapel Rockview Mennonite Church Youngstown, Ohio	O	1947	0	33	25	22	3	-24
Gladstone Mission Lee Heights Community Cleveland, Ohio	O	1947	0	231	321	280	41	38
Mennonite Community Church Ninth St. Mennonite Saginaw, Michigan	IM	1949	0	49	67	66	1	36
Camp Rehoboth Rehoboth Mennonite St. Anne, Illinois	I	1949	0	93	43	36	7	-53
Totals			**203**	**711**	**838**	**526**	**312**	

Observations on Figure 1

1. Of the 13 missions, seven are black or integrated; five are predominately white; three have closed; five have established another black church; one has taken a community rather than a denominational approach.

2. Estimated black membership in 1950 was 150. In 1980 it was 526, a gain of 376. Black membership has had a growth rate of 54 percent in a 30-year period, or an annual growth rate of nearly 5 percent.

3. Gladstone, now Lee Heights Community Church, assumed an interdenominational status when it relocated. Neither the majority of the members nor the church are considered members of the Mennonite Church. Approximately 40 people of the 321 are members of the Mennonite Church.

4. Lee Heights gained nearly half as many new members as the other 12 missions combined from 1950 to 1980.

5. In 1950, there was one black pastor. He was the first ordained black and was instrumental in establishing six of the 13 missions.

6. In Reading, Pennsylvania, a separate church, known as the Buttonwood

Fellowship, was established in 1971. This church is ministering primarily in the black community.

7. The average decadal growth rate of 10 churches is 38 percent while three of the 13 had an average 33 percent decline.

8. Blacks made up 63 percent of the total membership of the churches in 1980 with whites accounting for 37 percent. The first six eastern missions established between 1898 and 1950 had 21 percent black members and 79 percent white members, while the five established in the Midwest had 90 percent black and 10 percent white.

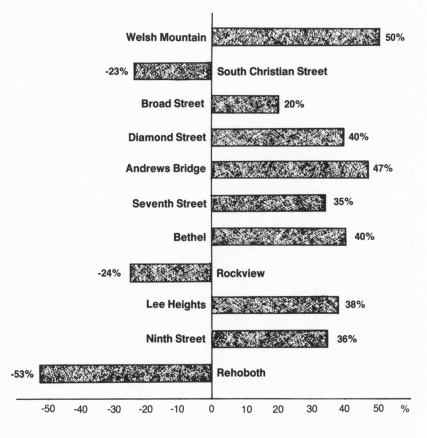

Figure 2: Decadal growth rate, 1970-1980
(Churches est. prior to 1950)

Figure 3: Black churches and black pastors

Average Annual Growth Rate .39%   Decadal Growth Rate 4%

Conf.	Date	Name	Location	Pastor	1970 T	1980 T	1980 B	1980 W
I	1893	Englewood	Chicago, Ill.	Louis Haggins	70	65	65	11
SW	1925	Calvary	Inglewood, Calif.	Hubert Brown	87	73	62	1
I	1944	Bethel	Chicago, Ill.	Leamon Sowell	40	56	55	3
O	1947	Rockview	Youngstown, Ohio	Charles McDowell	33	25	22	5
L	1949	Burnside	Bronx, N.Y.	Samuel Walters	21	20	15	1
IM	1949	Ninth St.	Saginaw, Mich.	Lee Arthur Lowery	49	67	66	
V	1952	Calvary	Newport News, Va.	Leslie Francisco	52	92	92	
V	1953	Norview	Norfolk, Va.	Wm. Vaughan	10	32	32	
SC	1957	Zion	Wichita, Kans.	Joe Holloway	55	20	20	
O	1962	Burnside	Columbus, Ohio	Warren Kelly	19	27	27	
IN	1965	North Side	Omaha, Nebr.	John Moore	37	15	15	
L	1968	Bible Fellowship	New Haven, Conn.			78	71	7
O	1970	University-Euclid	Cleveland, Ohio	Warner Jackson	41	43	43	
L	1971	Buttonwood	Reading, Pa.	Sam Brown		19	17	2
L/AF	1979	Mizpah	Estel Manor, N.J.	Fred Pittman		6	6	
SW	1980	Family	Los Angeles, Calif.	Oscar Price		28	24	4
Total						**666**	**632**	**34**

T: Total
B: Black
W: White

Figure 4: Integrated churches and black pastors

	Average Annual Growth Rate .68%			Decadal Growth Rate 7%				
					Membership			
					1970	1980		
Conf.	Date	Name	Location	Pastor	T	T	B	W
IM	1926	Peace Community	Detroit, Mich.	Julius Dotson	23	69	47	22
F	1949	Bristol	Philadelphia, Pa.	Raymond Jackson	23	18	5	13
F	1959	Bethel	Norristown, Pa.	Herman Douglas	13	66	51	15
IM	1961	Community	South Bend, Ind.	Al Brown	46	18	9	9
F	1962	Garden Chapel	Dover, N.J.	Jessie Adams		15	4	11
L	1970	Peabody	Washington, D.C.	George Richards	10	26	12	14
Total						212	128	84

Figure 5: Black churches and white pastors

	Average Annual Growth Rate .58%			Decadal Growth Rate 6%				
					Membership			
					1970	1980		
Conf.	Date	Name	Location	Pastor	T	T	B	W
Indep	1947	Lee Heights	Cleveland, Ohio	Vern Miller	231	321	280	41
I	1949	Rehoboth	St. Anne, Ill.	Mark Lehman	93	43	36	7
SE	1952	College Hill	Tampa, Fla.	George Stoltzfus	42	44	37	7
IM	1955	Grace Chapel	Saginaw, Mich.	John P. Wenger	32	56	52	4
SC	1958	Bethesda	St. Louis, Mo.	Jonas Miller	97	50	46	4
SE	1959	Newtown Chapel	Sarasota, Fla.	Mervin Shirk	40	50	41	9
L	1969	Good Shepherd	Bronx, N.Y.	Gene Shelly	16	23	20	3
Total						587	512	75

Figure 6: Integrated churches and white pastors

					Average Annual Growth Rate 2.01%	Decadal Growth Rate 22%		
					Membership			
					1970	1980		
Conf.	Date	Name	Location	Pastor	T	T	B	W
L	1933	South Christian St.	Lancaster, Pa.	L. Weaver	65	50	18	32
L	1935	Diamond St.	Philadelphia, Pa.	Freeman Miller	42	59	31	28
L	1946	Newlinville	Atglen, Pa.	Harold Engle	23	34	11	23
L	1950	Locust Lane	Harrisburg, Pa.	Glen Zeager	25	74	32	42
L	1951	Glad Tidings	Bronx, N.Y.	J. Bauman	57	28	6	22
L	1951	Hamilton St.	Harrisburg, Pa.	Robert Garber	11	10	7	3
L	1954	Seventh Ave.	New York, N.Y.	Gerald Keener	30	28	17	11
F	1954	Ambler	Ambler, Pa.	Berry Loop	34	67	13	54
IM	1954	Fairhaven	Ft. Wayne, Ind.	Earl Eberly	34	55	13	42
L	1954	Lincoln	Oxford, Pa.	J. Harnish	33	39	13	26
AC	1957	Friendship	Bronx, N.Y.	Mervin Horst	96	55	10	23W 22H
L	1958	Oak Drive	Atmore, Ala.	J. Huber	8	13	8	5
SW	1958	L.A. Fellowship	Los Angeles, Calif.	Leo Egli	40	58	40	18
SE	1960	Menn. Fellowship	Anderson, S.C.	Wilbur Lentz	6	44	12	32
L	1960	Mobile Menn.	Mobile, Ala.	J. Landis	4	7	2	5
SE	1960	Berea	Atlanta, Ga.	H. Shirk	42	49	10	39
SE	1961	First Menn.	St. Petersburg, Fla.	H. Weltz	21	25	4	21
OH	1962	Berean	Youngstown, Ohio	F. Augsburger	31	40	20	20
AC	1977	S. Coatesville	Coatesville, Pa.	M. Stoltzfus		12	6	6
L	1978	Aisquith	Baltimore, Md.	L. Zimmerman		19	11	8
Total					766		284	482

Figure 7: White churches and black members

| | | | | | Membership | | | |
| | | | | | 1970 | 1980 | | |
Conf.	Date	Name	Location	Pastor	T	T	B	W
				Average Annual Growth Rate 1.67%		Decadal Growth Rate 18%		
A	1790	Masontown	Masontown, Pa.	C. W. Opel	77	74	8	66
L	1898	Welsh Mt.	New Holland, Pa.	M. Leaman	36	54	6	48
O	1904	First Menn.	Canton, Ohio		67	93	7	86
F	1919	First Menn.	Norristown, Pa.	P. Hackman	56	58	10	48
L	1928	Coatesville	Coatesville, Pa.	E. Graybill	34	28	1	27
V	1935	Broad St.	Harrisonburg, Va.	Kenneth Handrich	40	48	4	44
L	1935	Steelton	Steelton, Pa.	D. W. Erb	108	104	9	95
OQ	1937	Warden Park	Toronto, Ont. Canada	J. Hess	62	100	7	93
L	1938	S. Seventh Street	Reading, Pa.	J. H. Good	58	65	6	59
L	1938	Andrews Bridge	Christiana, Pa.	E. H. Ranck	34	50	2	48
L	1954	Herr St.	Harrisburg, Pa.	H. H. Lefever	21	26	3	23
L	1954	Tidings of Peace	York, Pa.	M. Sell	21	11	2	9
L	1957	Norma	Bridgeton, N.J.	J. G. Miller	20	32	2	30
L	1962	Friendship	Salem, N.Y.	D. Lapp	3	9	1	8
Total						752	68	684

Figure 8: 1970-1980 decadal growth rate of black/integrated churches planted prior to 1970

No. Churches	1970	1980	AAGR	DGR
12 BC - B/P	514	535	.39%	4%
7 BC - W/P	551	587	.58%	6%
5 IC - B/P	115	197	.68%	7%
18 IC - W/P	602	735	2.0%	22%
42 Total	1,782	2,054	1.41%	15%
14 WC with BM	637	752	1.67%	18%
56 Total	2,419	2,806	1.50%	16%

Figure 9: 1970-1980 decadal growth rate percentages

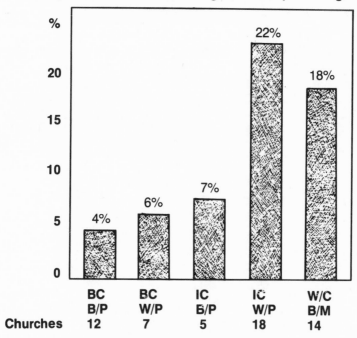

| Churches | BC B/P 12 | BC W/P 7 | IC B/P 5 | IC W/P 18 | W/C B/M 14 |

Figure 10: Average decadal growth rate of black/integrated churches

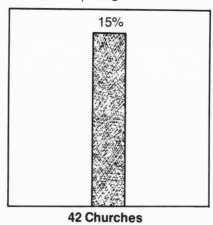

42 Churches

Figure 11: Dates black/integrated churches planted

	Prior to 40s	40s	50s	60s	70s	80s
BC-B/P	2	4	3	3	3	1
BC-W/P		2	4	1		
IC-B/P	1	1	1	2	2	
IC-W/P	2	1	10	5	1	
Total	5	8	18	11	6	1
	10%	16%	37%	22%	12%	2%

Figure 12: Dates black/integrated churches planted; percentages

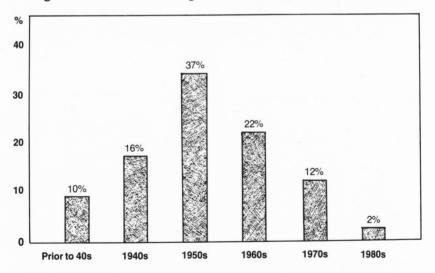

Figure 13: Membership size of black churches

	1-25	26-50	51-75	76-100	101-200	201+
BC-B/P	6	4	4	2		
BC-W/P	1	4	1			1
IC-B/P	4	1	2			
IC-W/P	5	8	6			
Totals	**16**	**17**	**13**	**2**		**1**
	33%	**35%**	**26%**	**4%**		**2%**

Figure 14: Membership size of black churches; percentages

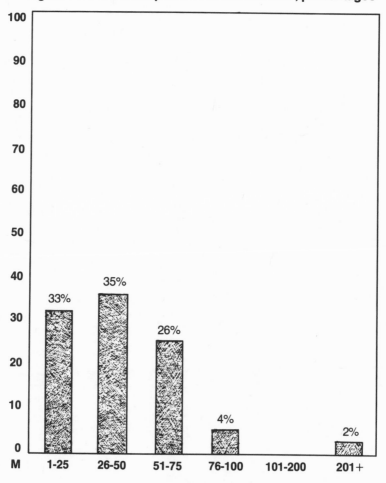

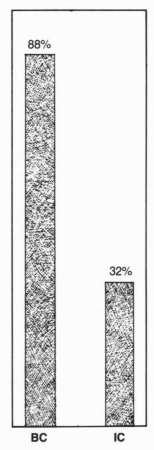

**Figure 15: Distribution
of black membership
in black and integrated
churches**

88%

32%

BC   IC

Figure 16: Pastoral leadership of black/integrated churches

		Membership		
	No.	T	B	W
BC-B/P	16	666	632	34
BC-W/P	7	587	512	75
IC-B/P	6	212	128	84
IC-W/P	20	766	284	482
Totals	**49**	**2,231**	**1,556**	**675**

Figure 17: Black membership by conferences

Conf.	Black or Integrated Churches	White Churches	Membership B	W
A	1	36	14	3,563
AC	2	39	16	3,995
F	4	46	83	5,969
I	3	37	156	4,016
IM	5	101	187	12,071
IN	1	41	15	4,727
L	16	190	323	16,319
OQ		37	7	4,792
O	5	80	399	11,411
SC	2	47	66	3,971
SE	5	20	92	1,512
SW	3	14	138	913
V	2	66	128	5,279

Thirteen out of 35 conferences, or 37 percent, have black membership. Sixty-three percent of Mennonite Church conferences have no black members.

NOTES

Chapter 1
1. John Runcie, "The Black Culture Movement and the Black Community," American Studies 10,2 (1976) p. 185.
2. Ibid.
3. Ibid.
4. Benjamin Elijah Mays, *The Negro's Church* (New York: Russell and Russell), 1969.
5. Runcie, p. 186.
6. Ibid. p. 187.
7. Ibid. p. 188.
8. Ibid. p. 190.
9. Ibid. p. 190.
10. Ibid. p. 214.

Chapter 2
1. Carter G. Woodson, *The History of the Negro Church* (Washington, D.C.: The Associates Publishers, 1921, 1945, p. 2.
2. Richard C. Wade, "Beyond the Master's Eyes," in *The Black Church in America* (New York: Basic Books, 1971, pp. 62-73.
3. Emmanual L. McCall, *The Black Christian Experience* (Nashville: Broadman Press, 1972, p. 59.
4. Henry Mitchell, *Black Belief* (New York: Harper and Row, 1975), p. 22.
5. Franklin E. Frazier, *The Negro Church in America* (New York: Schocken Books, 1963, p. 16.
6. Richard I. McKinney, "The Black Church," in *Harvard Theological Review*, 64 (1971), p. 455.
7. Ibid. p. 458.
8. Frazier, p. 30.
9. McKinney, p. 464.
10. Frazier, p. 43.
11. McKinney, p. 467.
12. H. A. Jackson, "Religious Symbols and Black Experience," in *Religion in Life* 41, Spring 1972, pp. 29-36, 33.

INDEX

THE AUTHOR

Le Roy Bechler has spent nearly thirty years in cross-cultural ministry as a church planter and pastor in the ghettos of Chicago, Illinois; Saginaw, Michigan; and Los Angeles, California. He helped found the indigenous Calvary Christian School at Inglewood, California, which has an enrollment of over 225 students.

Born in Pigeon, Michigan, Bechler received his B.A. in religious education from Hesston College, Hesston, Kansas. He earned a Master's degree in missiology from Fuller Theological Seminary's School of World Missions, Pasadena, California. He has also done graduate work at Atlanta University, Atlanta, Georgia, and at Associated Mennonite Biblical Seminaries, Elkhart, Indiana.

Le Roy and his wife, Irene (Springer), attend the Bayshore Mennonite Church, Sarasota, Florida. They are the parents of one daughter, Kathleen Lechlitner, and of two sons, Kent L. and Curt T.

Ordained to the ministry in 1950, Bechler served as church planter in Saginaw, Michigan, from 1950 to 1960. He was called to the Calvary Mennonite Church in Los Angeles to provide pastoral leadership in a racially changing community from 1961 to 1979.

He was director of church extension of the Southwest Mennonite Conference, chairman of the Greater Los Angeles Mennonite Ministers' Council, and president of the Inglewood Ministerial Association, as well as a member of the Black Council of the Mennonite Church for four years.

Bechler has held many church growth diagnostic seminars and has served on the churchwide Church Growth/Evangelism Resource Team. Since 1984 he is Home Missions secretary of the Southeast Mennonite Convention and is director of its Pastoral Training Program.